Signing the Scriptures

YEAR B

A Starting Point
for Interpreting
the Sunday Readings
for the Deaf

Joan Blake

LTP
LITURGY
TRAINING
PUBLICATIONS

SIGNING THE SCRIPTURES: A STARTING POINT FOR
INTERPRETING THE SUNDAY READINGS FOR THE DEAF,
YEAR B © 2005 Archdiocese of Chicago: Liturgy
Training Publications, 1800 North Hermitage Avenue,
Chicago IL 60622-1101; 1-800-933-1800, fax 1-800-
933-7094, e-mail orders@ltp.org. All rights reserved.
See our website at www.ltp.org.

Audrey Novak Riley was the production editor of this
book. The design is by M. Urgo, and the typesetting was
done by Kari Nicholls in Sabon and Lithos. Cover photo
© 2003 Photos.com.

Printed in the United States of America.

Library of Congress Control Number 2005930694

ISBN 1-56854-592-4

SIGNB

CONTENTS

Introduction	v
Symbols	vi
First Sunday of Advent	1
Second Sunday of Advent	3
Third Sunday of Advent	5
Fourth Sunday of Advent	7
Christmas Vigil	10
Christmas, Midnight Mass	13
Christmas, Mass during the Day	15
Holy Family	17
Blessed Virgin Mary, Mother of God	21
Epiphany of the Lord	23
Baptism of the Lord	25
Ash Wednesday	28
First Sunday of Lent	30
Second Sunday of Lent	32
Third Sunday of Lent	34
Third Sunday of Lent, Year A	36
Fourth Sunday of Lent	39
Fourth Sunday of Lent, Year A	41
Fifth Sunday of Lent	44
Fifth Sunday of Lent, Year A	46
Palm Sunday of the Lord's Passion	49
Holy Thursday	56
Good Friday	58
Easter Vigil	66
Easter Sunday	76
Second Sunday of Easter	78
Third Sunday of Easter	80
Fourth Sunday of Easter	82
Fifth Sunday of Easter	84
Sixth Sunday of Easter	86
Ascension of the Lord	88
Seventh Sunday of Easter	91
Pentecost Sunday	93
Holy Trinity	96
Body and Blood of Christ	98
Second Sunday in Ordinary Time	100
Third Sunday in Ordinary Time	102
Fourth Sunday in Ordinary Time	104
Fifth Sunday in Ordinary Time	106

Sixth Sunday in Ordinary Time	108
Seventh Sunday in Ordinary Time	110
Eighth Sunday in Ordinary Time	112
Ninth Sunday in Ordinary Time	114
Tenth Sunday in Ordinary Time	116
Eleventh Sunday in Ordinary Time	119
Twelfth Sunday in Ordinary Time	121
Thirteenth Sunday in Ordinary Time	123
Fourteenth Sunday in Ordinary Time	125
Fifteenth Sunday in Ordinary Time	127
Sixteenth Sunday in Ordinary Time	129
Seventeenth Sunday in Ordinary Time	131
Eighteenth Sunday in Ordinary Time	133
Nineteenth Sunday in Ordinary Time	135
Twentieth Sunday in Ordinary Time	137
Twenty-first Sunday in Ordinary Time	139
Twenty-second Sunday in Ordinary Time	141
Twenty-third Sunday in Ordinary Time	143
Twenty-fourth Sunday in Ordinary Time	145
Twenty-fifth Sunday in Ordinary Time	147
Twenty-sixth Sunday in Ordinary Time	149
Twenty-seventh Sunday in Ordinary Time	151
Twenty-eighth Sunday in Ordinary Time	153
Twenty-ninth Sunday in Ordinary Time	155
Thirtieth Sunday in Ordinary Time	157
Thirty-first Sunday in Ordinary Time	159
Thirty-second Sunday in Ordinary Time	161
Thirty-third Sunday in Ordinary Time	163
Christ the King	165
Presentation of the Lord	167
Nativity of John the Baptist	169
Saints Peter and Paul, Apostles	171
Transfiguration of the Lord	173
Assumption of the Blessed Virgin Mary	175
Exaltation of the Holy Cross	177
All Saints	179
Dedication of the Lateran Basilica	181
Immaculate Conception	183
Glossary of Signs	185
Index of Scriptures	188

INTRODUCTION

Welcome to *Signing the Scriptures: A Starting Point for Interpreting the Sunday Readings for the Deaf, Year B*. If you are new to religious interpreting, or even if you're an old hand at it but sometimes find yourself struggling with the complex sentences and figurative language of the Scriptures, this book was written for you. It has been developed over twenty years of interpreting the three-year cycle of the Roman Catholic *Lectionary for Mass*, but it is still a work in progress. The work won't be finished until you take it, revise it, adapt it to your personal understanding and style, and make it your own. These glosses are not intended to be used "as is." It may happen that you can sign some of the readings straight out of the book, but my hope is that you will use these suggestions as a stimulus to help you move away from word-for-word English into a more conceptual framework, according to the language preference of your audience.

To make it easier to sign the glosses, I have tried to be consistent in labeling the signs with the standard English words that are normally found in an ASL/English dictionary. Occasionally I create my own English gloss for an idiomatic sign, and these can be found in the glossary at the back of the book. In addition, there is a list of symbols to help you understand the "stage directions." These symbols were originally used to help me remember what I had practiced (I hope you practice the readings before you get to church!)—where I had decided to place the characters, what direction they were going to move, which hand I wanted to use for a specific sign, and so on. I included them in this book, not to tell you how to set up your signing space, but to remind you to set it up, and to suggest one way of doing it.

Feel free to make any revisions you consider necessary to make your interpretation clear and in conformity with your own religious tradition. This is a workbook, and my hope is that you will use it in whatever way is most helpful to you.

For a more in-depth discussion of ways to apply ASL techniques to Scripture interpretations, please see the companion video, *Tips and Techniques for Signing the Scriptures*.

SYMBOLS

\# followed by a word in all caps, for example, #ALL • use fingerspelled loan sign

++ • reduplicate the sign two or more times

cl:_ _ • use the given handshapes to show the shape, size, or movement of the named object

? before a sentence • a question mark in the air

?? • crook index finger into a little question mark several times

Exclamation point after a word in the middle of a sentence • sign that word strongly

Numbers in parentheses • list on fingers

Underlined words, for example, Peter • fingerspell the word in the normal way

Words in brackets • may be omitted

Words with a hyphen (-) between, for example, two-of-them • use one sign for the phrase

Words with a tilde (~) between, for example, true~work • two signs flow together

(lh), (rh), (bh) • left hand, right hand, both hands

(l), (r) • place that sign on the left or the right

hon • honorific. Open hand, palm up, indicates person being referred to

^^ • indicates pronoun. Legs

Words in parentheses, for example, (on fingers) • directions to interpreter

First Sunday of Advent

BOOK OF THE PROPHET ISAIAH (63:16–17, 19; 64:2–7)

Lord, you our Father true, our Savior forever. You allow us back-slide—why? You influence-it heart hard, honor you not—for-for? Please come #BACK, your people save. I wish heaven open, mountain shake, you come-down (cl:1), action wonderful things no person see, hear, up-to-now. Other god action wonderful things, nothing! Only you. We action right, I wish you notice; your law I wish we obey. You angry; we sinners true. We #ALL dirty, our good work compare dirty clothes. We guilty #ALL. Who pray-to you? None. Who cherish you? None. Your face you turn-away-cover. We sin; you give-up, abandon-there. But Lord, you our Father true. You finish make us, love us.

Word his Lord.

RESPONSORIAL PSALM (80:2–3, 15–16, 18–19)

Lord, help-us look-at-you, your face see, save-us.

You care-for us, please pay-attention / there heaven shine-down
Your power enthusiastic / come save us.

Again, Lord God / there heaven, look-down,
People you cherish, please care-for / you yourself give-them strong.

People good you help / those people you make strong
We avoid you not / new life give-us, your name we depend-on.

FIRST LETTER OF PAUL TO THE CORINTHIANS (1:3–9)

Grace and peace from God Father and from Lord Jesus Christ, I-give-you. I thank++ God, reason? He finish give-you skill speak++, know++. I past teach-you about Christ, now you prove—How?

Every spirit gift from God you have now, during you wait-for Lord Jesus come again. He give-you strong until last day; finish, happen Jesus come (cl:1), you clean, have sin none. God himself faithful. He summon you united-to his son, Jesus Christ our Lord.

Word his Lord.

GOSPEL ACCLAMATION

Alleluia

Lord, please love-us, save-us.

HOLY GOSPEL ACCORDING TO MARK (13:33–37)

Jesus tell apostles: Hey, continue careful++, watch++—Why? Time Lord come, you don't-know. Compare man travel-away. He tell each servant his++ responsibility; man there gate guard, he-tell-him "Warning, eyes-wide-open, watch++." Finish, off-he-goes. Same you. Time boss #BACK you don't-know, maybe sunset, midnight, early-morning, sunrise—don't-know. Maybe show-up, see you sound-asleep, oh-I-see. I inform-all, continue eyes-wide-open, ready.

Gospel his Lord.

Second Sunday of Advent

BOOK OF THE PROPHET ISAIAH (40:1–5, 9–11)

God says, My people there++, comfort you-give-them. Jerusalem there, speak-to-it kindly, inform-it time-period slavery finished, guilt forgive. Each sin, Lord finish punish twice. Someone shout: There desert, make way for Lord. Make road straight, wide, for God. Every valley raise-up, every hill flatten, rough become smooth. Finish, Lord glory show for #ALL people see. Lord promise.

Jerusalem, go-to mountain, happy <u>news</u> inform-all, shout loud. Tell cities there++ quote, "Here God! He come-down (cl:1) full power, Lord God himself control strong. He bring-down give-you, he bring-down pay fair. People he care-for compare shepherd care-for (sheep); people he gather, hold-in-arms (mime), lead safe."

Word his Lord.

RESPONSORIAL PSALM (85:9–10, 11–12, 13–14)

Lord, your kindness show-us, please save-us.

God speak, I pay-attention / Lord announce peace for his people
Those honor-him, he near-future save-them / glory give-to their land.

Kindness, honest connect / judge~fair, peace harmonize
Honest earth have / judge~fair itself look-down.

Lord himself bless us / land grow, grow plenty
God himself judge fair / prepare for future come-down.

SECOND LETTER OF PETER (3:8–14)

Important remember; for Lord, one day equal same 1,000 years, same. Lord promise—he postpone++? No-wave. He patient wait-for #ALL people sorry, sin stop. One lose, he don't-want. Happen day

Lord come (cl:1), not~expect. Sky dissolve, loud-noise, everything fire destroy; here earth, people actions show clear. Means you must live how? Holy, enthusiastic wait-for day Lord come. That day, sky? fire destroy; earth? fire dissolve. We wait-for sky new, earth new, there everything good. During wait, try live right, sin none, peace united God.

Word his Lord.

GOSPEL ACCLAMATION

Alleluia

Prepare way for Lord, make straight-way
#ALL people he save will.

HOLY GOSPEL ACCORDING TO MARK (1:1–8)

Now open start gospel story Jesus Christ, son his God. Prophet Isaiah long-ago write: Preacher God send early, they prepare way for Messiah. There desert someone shout, quote, "Make way for Lord."

John Baptizer show-up there desert. He preach what? "Yourself immerse must, show you sorry; finish, God forgive-you." Many people all-over-area flock-to-him, sin confess, immerse. John clothes camel hair, belt. He eat grasshopper bug and honey. He preach++ what? Quote, "Other person will come (cl:1), himself important than me. I kneel-down, his shoes touch, not worthy enough me. I recent immerse you there water. He will influence-you Holy Spirit."

Gospel his Lord.

Third Sunday of Advent

BOOK OF THE PROPHET ISAIAH (61:1–2, 10–11)

Lord God, his spirit inspire me, why(?) Lord finish choose-me. Those people humble, he send me inform-them happy; those people heart-crushed, heal; those people slave, free; stuck prison, out free. I announce year special from Lord, day full judge-fair from God.

I celebrate Lord; my soul he give-me happy. He save me, judge right. I compare <u>groom</u>, clothes fancy; <u>or</u> I compare <u>bride</u> shiny++ (from crown, necklace, ring). Earth grow++ flowers, people see; same Lord God give judge-fair and praise, show-around #ALL nations.

Word his Lord.

RESPONSORIAL PSALM (Luke 1:46–48, 49–50, 53–54)

My soul celebrate connect-to God.

My soul announce Lord true wonderful /
my spirit celebrate connect-to God my Savior
Myself his humble servant, he look-at-me /
from-now-on #ALL people honor me

God finish wonderful action for me / his name true holy
People honor-him, he mercy-them / up-to-now, forever.

People hungry, he give-them satisfied / people rich, he shoo-away, give-them nothing
His humble people he help / he promise mercy-them, he remember.

FIRST LETTER OF PAUL TO THE THESSALONIANS (5:16–24)

(1) Celebrate always, (2) pray continue, (3) thank++ God. These-three-things (on fingers), God want. Prophet story, hate not. Everything test, analyze, investigate. Suppose good, save; bad, reject.

I pray God, himself full peace, he-influence-you holy perfect. I pray your body, soul he save, protect; continue sin none until Lord Jesus Christ come. God summon us; we trust him save us can he.

Word his Lord.

GOSPEL ACCLAMATION

Alleluia

God his spirit inspire me,
he send me for people poor, good #NEWS inform-them.

HOLY GOSPEL ACCORDING TO JOHN (1:6–8, 19–28)

Man name John, God send-him for teach about Jesus, help people believe. But only teach about Jesus. Himself Jesus not.

Jew group send leaders few go-to [John], question-him, "Who you?" John answer, "Messiah not, me." "? You Elijah?" "No." "Prophet?" "No." (Jews) "Well, tell us who, there Jerusalem people we inform can. What say you?" John answered, use word same prophet Isaiah, "I myself someone here desert, shout: Make way for Lord."

Jews more question-him: "You Messiah not, Elijah not, prophet not, but you immerse people—why?" John tell-them, "I use water immerse. But other person out-there, you don't-know who, he come later—his shoes touch, I not worthy enough."

That story happen there Bethany, near river Jordan, there people John baptize.

Gospel his Lord.

Fourth Sunday of Advent

SECOND BOOK OF SAMUEL (7:1–5, 8–12, 14, 16)

King David live house comfortable. War-right, war-left dissolve finish, rest, tell prophet name Nathan, "I live house wood fine-wiggle, God his Ten Commandments (cl:[ ]) write, left-there tent." Nathan answered, "#Do-do, think-self. God support-you." But, same night, Nathan sleep, dream, Lord tell-him: Go, tell David, Lord says, "Build house for me, you want? Long-ago, you shepherd, I choose you, put-you rule my people Israel. You group-travel, I accompany; your enemy, I destroy. Cause-you famous will I; prepare place for my people Israel move, settle, peace. Bad enemy up-to-now bother++, finish, no more. I give-you peace, rest. Establish house for you will I. Your house, your kingdom continue forever; your rule stand-strong."

Word his Lord.

RESPONSORIAL PSALM (89:2–3, 4–5, 27, 29)

Forever I sing, Lord himself good.

Lord his promise, I sing forever / for people future I announce he faithful
God he kind up-to-now forever / there heaven he prove himself faithful.

God says, "I finish promise my special person / himself David my servant
Forever your children descendents I support / your control continue forever."

David will say, "You (God) my father / my God, my support, my Savior."
Forever God kind-to-him / God promise continue stand-strong.

LETTER OF PAUL TO ROMANS (16:25–27)

God give-you strong can, how? Follow gospel about Jesus Christ. God his secret hide up-to-now, but now clear explain through writing theirs prophets. God command what? Gospel inform #ALL people—for-for? They believe, obey can. God himself true wise. Glory give-him with Jesus Christ forever. Amen (in palm)!

Word his Lord.

GOSPEL ACCLAMATION

Alleluia

Emmanuel, #ALL people you give-them happy
Come, save us. Lord Jesus, come.

or

Myself Lord his servant
Your recent story, I accept.

HOLY GOSPEL ACCORDING TO LUKE (1:26–38)

Angel name <u>Gabriel</u>, God send-him touch town name <u>Nazareth</u>, visit virgin herself engaged man name <u>Joseph</u>, he family <u>David</u> descended. Virgin, her name <u>Mary</u>. Angel meet-her, said, "Celebrate! God with you, bless you special want!" Mary puzzled, not-understand. (Angel) "Fear, no-wave. God choose you (hon) special—for-for? You will pregnant, born son, name-him Jesus. Son, whew, honor! Name-him, quote, 'son his most elevated.' Lord God give-him control same <u>David</u>, his ancestor. He control Israel people forever."

Mary question, "Pregnant how? Married not-yet me." (Angel) "Holy Spirit touch influence you will, cause pregnant—baby true~work Son his God. Know-that your cousin <u>Elizabeth</u>, herself old, now pregnant. People think she pregnant can't (^), now what? pregnant six months. See? God expert can." (Mary) "Serve Lord, I willing. You recent story, I accept." Finish, angel depart~dissolve.

Gospel his Lord.

Christmas Vigil

BOOK OF THE PROPHET ISAIAH (62:1–5)

<u>Zion</u> I love, silent refuse me. Jerusalem I love, I talk continue until its good action shines compare sunrise, until its success shows compare candle. Your success, #ALL nations will see; your glory, #ALL kings will see. Lord himself give-you name new. You compare beautiful crown for God. Past, people name-you, quote, "Abandoned"; your land they name, quote, "Empty." But now people name-you, quote, "God cherish"; your land they name, quote, "God wife." Lord love you, your land want marry. Pretty girl, young man marry; same God marry you. Wife, husband cherish; same God cherish you.

Word his Lord.

RESPONSORIAL PSALM (89:4–5, 16–17, 27, 29)

Forever I sing, Lord himself good

God say, "My special person I finish promise / himself <u>David</u> my servant.
Your family I support generations / your kingdom continue forever."

Those people, good news they know, happy they / they walk face-to-face (God)
Your name they hear, happy / you judge fair, bless-them.

<u>David</u> will say, "Yourself my Father / my God, my support, my Savior."
God kindness continue forever / God promise stand-strong.

ACTS OF THE APOSTLES (13:16–17, 22–25)

Synagogue (s-y like church) Paul enter, said, "Israel people, #ALL honor God, pay-attention-me. Long-ago, our ancestor~group,

God choose. During time there Egypt, he help them; later, he lead them out safe. God choose <u>David</u> become king, why? He said, "<u>David</u> have heart same-as-mine, follow my want will he." Now generations-forward, born Jesus, himself savior for Israel. <u>John</u> prepare Israel people for Jesus arrive, how? Immerse, change life. <u>John</u> preach, say, "Myself Messiah not. Other man come will. Touch his shoes, I not worthy enough."

Word his Lord.

GOSPEL ACCLAMATION

Alleluia

Tomorrow, here earth sin, God destroy,
Savior for world take-up control will.

HOLY GOSPEL ACCORDING TO MATTHEW (1:1–25)

(Shorter: omit text in brackets)

[Jesus, his pass-down-generations, begin <u>Abraham</u> up-till-now:
<u>Abraham</u> born <u>Isaac</u>, pass-to <u>Jacob</u>,
pass-to <u>Judah</u> and brother,
pass-to <u>Perez</u> and <u>Zerah</u>, their mother <u>Tamar</u>,
pass-to <u>Hezron</u>, pass-to <u>Ram</u>,
pass-to <u>Amminadab</u>, pass-to <u>Nahshon</u>
pass-to <u>Salmon</u>, pass-to <u>Boaz</u>, his mother <u>Rahab</u>,
pass-to <u>Obed</u>, his mother <u>Ruth</u>
pass-to <u>Jesse</u>, pass-to King <u>David</u>.

<u>David</u> born <u>Solomon</u>, his mother ex-wife <u>Uriah</u>,
pass-to <u>Rehoboam</u>, pass-to <u>Abijah</u>,
pass-to <u>Asaph</u>, pass-to <u>Jehoshaphat</u>,
pass-to <u>Joram</u>, pass-to <u>Uzziah</u>,
pass-to <u>Jotham</u>, pass-to <u>Ahaz</u>
pass-to <u>Hezekiah</u>, pass-to <u>Manasseh</u>
pass-to <u>Amos</u>, pass-to <u>Josiah</u>,

pass-to Jechoniah and brother during time-period slave there Babylon. Slave time-period finish, Jechoniah born Shealtiel,
pass-to Zerubbabel, pass-to Abiud,
pass-to Eliakim, pass-to Azor,
pass-to Zadok, pass-to Achim
pass-to Eliud, pass-to Eleazar
pass-to Matthan, pass-to Jacob, his son Joseph, that-one Mary marry. She, Mary, born Jesus Christ.

Altogether generations how-many? Abraham to David, fourteen. David to time-period slave, fourteen. Time-period slave to Jesus born, fourteen.]

Now story Jesus born: His mother Mary engage man name Joseph, understand, married not-yet, herself hit pregnant, how? Holy Spirit cause. Joseph good man, punish her don't-want; private divorce decide. Wrong, dream, angel show-up, tell-him, "Fear none, go-ahead marry; Mary pregnant how? Holy Spirit. She will born son. Name-him Jesus must you, why? His people he save."

Recent story happen for-for? Long-ago prophet write: "Virgin will hit pregnant, born son, name-him Emmanuel." [Word means, "God with us."]

Joseph wake-up, obey angel, two-of-them marry. Two-of-them sex never until born son, name Jesus.

Gospel his Lord.

CHRISTMAS, MIDNIGHT MASS

BOOK OF THE PROPHET ISAIAH (9:1–3, 5–6)

People past live dark, now see bright-light; past live land obscure, now light-shine-down. God give-them happy, celebrate. They celebrate face-to-face God same harvest time, excited money share-around. Why? Their burden, their suffering, God destroy same past, [day of Midian]. Time-period war, finished. Clothes bloody, fire~dissolve.

Now, baby born; son God give-us. He take control will. They name-him, quote, "(1) Wonderful Counselor, (2) God-Hero, (3) Father Forever, (4) Prince (of) Peace." His kingdom huge, have peace forever. David his kingdom, he (son) support continue, judge fair now and forever. Lord enthusiastic action these-things (on fingers).

Word his Lord.

RESPONSORIAL PSALM (96:1–2, 2–3, 11–12, 13)

Today born our Savior, Christ Lord.

New song sign-ASL-to Lord / sing for Lord, #ALL people
Sing for Lord / his name honor.

Every-day, announce he save us / his glory inform #ALL people
All-over world / his wonderful work announce.

(1) Heaven happy, earth celebrate / (2) ocean, fish sing, happy
(3) Field, animals celebrate / (4) #ALL trees excited, happy.

They (on fingers) happy why? Lord finish come /
he come for control take-up
World, he control fair-around / people, he control faithful.

LETTER OF PAUL TO TITUS (2:11–14)

God his grace now here, for save #ALL people. Grace teach-us what? Sin, world thirst, push-aside; live right, holy during wait, hope see glory God and Jesus, our Savior. Jesus himself sacrifice die for us, save us, our sin forgive; now we his people true; action right, we enthusiastic.

Word his Lord.

GOSPEL ACCLAMATION

Alleluia

I inform-you wonderful happen:
Today born Savior, Christ Lord.

HOLY GOSPEL ACCORDING TO LUKE (2:1–14)

Long-ago, controller name Caesar Augustus order #ALL people all-over count. So each person go-to town that-one his family generations-back start. Joseph live there Nazareth, go-to town name Bethlehem—reason? Himself family David descend—wife Mary, two-of-them go, understand, Mary herself pregnant. During there, happen time give-birth baby. Mary give-birth, cloth wrap-up, manger lay-him-in—Why? There house travelers stay all-night, full, room have none.

Near area, shepherds work watch all-night. Angel from Lord show-up, glory shine-down (bh); they afraid! Angel tell-them, "Afraid, nothing. I inform-you wonderful happen, good #NEWS for #ALL people. Today, recent there Bethlehem, born Savior, himself Messiah, Lord. Proof what? Manger, you go-to-it, notice baby, cloth wrap-up, lay-in." Wrong, angels many! hordes sing praise God, quote, "Glory give-to God heaven, peace touch earth for people he cherish."

Gospel his Lord.

Christmas, Mass During the Day

BOOK OF THE PROPHET ISAIAH (52:7–10)

Person walk mountain, his feet cherish—why? That-one person good #NEWS bring, peace announce, inform happy, announce save, and tell #ALL people, "Your God true King!" Hey! Your prophet shout, together shout happy—why? They see, visualize: Zion, Lord again establish. Jerusalem, itself finish destroyed, now again sing happy—why? Lord his people he comfort; Jerusalem he save. Lord his holy power show, #ALL people see. His people, God save, #ALL countries see will.

Word his Lord.

RESPONSORIAL PSALM (98:1, 2–3, 3–4, 5–6)

All-over earth, people see God expert save.

New song sign-ASL-to Lord / he finish wonderful action
His right hand win succeed / himself mighty.

#ALL people Lord himself save / #ALL countries his judge~fair he show-around
He up-to-now kind, faithful / people Israel he cherish.

People all-over earth / finish see God save us
#ALL country sing happy for Lord / sign-ASL, praise.

Sing praise Lord with harp (cl) / song, voice, praise
Trumpet loud, music / happy sign-ASL-to Lord, King.

LETTER TO THE HEBREWS (1:1–6)

Long-ago, our ancestors God speak-to obscure—how? Prophet preach. Now, God speak-to us clear through his Son. God, with Jesus, two-of-them world, everything make, set-up, share equal.

Father his glory, Jesus show; two-of-them exact same, wrong none. Our sin, Son remove; finish, heaven go, sit, control with God. Angels, he beat (shot-h); their name, his name beat. ? God tell angel, "You my son; today I become your Father"?? No, never. Happen God his first-born Son send go-to world, he say, "#ALL angels worship him must."

Word his Lord.

GOSPEL ACCLAMATION

Alleluia

Now morning holy day
Come, #ALL people, worship Lord
Today earth, light shine-down.

HOLY GOSPEL ACCORDING TO JOHN (1:1–18)

Before world begin, before, Jesus himself with God, Jesus himself true~work God. Everything, he make++. Jesus give life; life cause light. Dark, no-matter, light shine, beat-it (shot-h). Man name John, God send, for-for? Inform people about Jesus. Himself Jesus not, but his duty teach about Jesus, that-one come, light give for world. World Jesus touch—world himself make—but world don't-know who he. People accept-him not. But people few accept-him; those, he give-them power become children his God. Suppose people believe his name, mother~father not~need. They born from God himself.

Jesus become human, live here earth. His glory we finish see, God his Son, full grace and honest. John preach about him, said, "Remember I tell-you other person come, himself important than me? That-one he." Jesus give-you grace increase++. Moses give law, but Jesus give grace, honest. See God, impossible; but Jesus himself show-you God.

Gospel his Lord.

Holy Family

BOOK OF GENESIS (15:1–6; 21:1–3)

Abraham, God inform-him, "Fear, no. I protect-you. Wonderful give-you will I." But Abraham said, "Lord, God, your gift-to-me worthless, why? Children have none. I die, my money leave who? My servant?" God tell-him, "No. Son will you, money leave-him." Lord lead Abraham outside, said, "See stars? Count possible? Impossible! Same children will you, count impossible." Abraham believe, faith. Lord look-at <u>Sarah</u>, promise succeed. <u>Sarah</u> hit pregnant, born son, two of them old no-matter. Son, Abraham name-him <u>Isaac</u>.

Word his Lord.

or

BOOK OF SIRACH (3:2–6, 12–14)

Father, Lord put-him-there, children honor must; mother, God give-her authority control son. Suppose person honor father, his sin God forgive; respect mother, wonderful things God reserve for him. Honor father, many children will you; happen you pray, God pay-attention. Person honor father, live from-now-on long; person comfort mother, that-one obey Lord. My son, suppose your father old, care-for him; cause-him grief not. Suppose father mind-weak, patient. Yourself strong, make-fun-of-him not. Why? You kind-to father, God remember. Later you sin, God forgive.

Word his Lord.

RESPONSORIAL PSALM (105:1–2, 3–4, 5–6, 8–9)

Lord promise, he remember forever.

Thank-you Lord, his name announce / his actions inform #ALL people
Sing-to God, praise sign-ASL / his wonderful work announce.

Glory honor his name / celebrate, search-for Lord
Trust Lord, he give-you strong / depend-on him always.

You people, Abraham descend, you serve him / you Israel people, he choose-you special
Lord himself our God / all-over earth, he expert judge.

His promise he remember forever / he promise for 1,000 generations
Long-ago he promise Abraham / he promise-to Israel.

LETTER TO THE HEBREWS (11:8, 11–12, 17–19)

Brother~sister, Abraham God order-him go-to place, he don't-know where, but patient~accept, go. Because he faith, possible he born son; understand he old, wife Sarah herself born baby can't (^). But trust God. Himself old, almost ready die, no-matter, he have descendants many, same stars many. Why? Abraham faith, willing his only son kill, sacrifice. God finish promise son will born many descendants, no-matter, kill willing. He (Abraham) believe God raise him (son) live again possible. (Note: Placement is important!)

Word his Lord.

or

LETTER OF PAUL TO THE COLOSSIANS (3:12–21)

God choose you special, holy, cherish. Now must you become mercy, (2) kind, (3) humble, (4) sweet, (5) patient. Accept each-other; forgive, complain++ push-aside, forgive, same Lord finish forgive you. Last, must you love—why? Love cause these-things (on fingers) become perfect. Christ his peace control your heart. You united-around, peace must you. Always thank-(God). Christ, his word important true; allow his word inspire you. Yourselves wise, teach each-other. Sing thanks-to God heart-express, psalm and holy songs sign-ASL-to-God. Any #do-do, no-matter talk, action—honor name Lord Jesus. Thank God Father through Jesus. [You wives, humble obey husband—why? Your duty. Husband, love wife, anger, hate none. Children, you-all obey parents every way—reason? Lord satisfy. Fathers, you-all bawl-out children, no-wave. They maybe feel discouraged.]

Word his Lord.

GOSPEL ACCLAMATION

Alleluia

Long-ago, God talk through prophet;
now he talk through son Jesus.

HOLY GOSPEL ACCORDING TO LUKE (2:22–40)

Mary, Joseph follow law Moses, baby Jesus bring-to Jerusalem, for-for? Offer-to God. Law require what? Every first-born boy offer-to-Lord must. Plus, parents must sacrifice birds two. Happen there Jerusalem man name Simeon, himself good, holy, he wait-for Messiah arrive. Holy Spirit inform-him what? He live until he see Messiah. Now, Holy Spirit tell-him temple go-to, see Mary, Joseph, Jesus. Baby he (Simeon) take-in-arms, praise God, said, "Now die peace can I, why? Your promise satisfied. Savior you send for #ALL people, light for non-Jews and glory for Jew people, I finish see."

Mary, Joseph listen, puzzled. Two-of-them Simeon bless, tell Mary, "This baby will grow-up, cause many people fail and many people succeed all-over Israel. People oppose-him will; and yourself suffer, for-for? People their thought++ show clear."

There temple have woman prophet name <u>Anna</u>, herself old. Long-ago she married, live with husband 7 years, husband die; she live alone up-to-now, now age 84. She frequented temple, all-day, all-night worship, fasting, pray. Now arrive, see baby, thank God; finish, she inform-all Jesus save Jerusalem will.

Law obey finish, family group-go #BACK home <u>Nazareth</u>. Baby grow-up, strong, wise; God his grace influence-him.

Gospel his Lord.

Blessed Virgin Mary, Mother of God

BOOK OF NUMBERS (6:22–27)

Moses Lord inform-him, quote, "Tell <u>Aaron</u> and his son bless Israel people how? Say: 'Lord bless you, protect you. Lord his face shine-down-on-you, mercy-you. Lord kind look-down kind, peace give-you.' Pray finish, bless-them will I."

Word his Lord.

RESPONSORIAL PSALM (67:2–3, 5, 6, 8)

God please mercy-me, bless-me.

God please mercy-me, bless-me / his face shine-down-on-me
Finish, his action here we know / he save us, #ALL people know.

#ALL people / celebrate happy—why?
Because God control-them fair / #ALL people he lead right.

#ALL people praise-you God / #ALL countries praise you
God please bless us, / #ALL people see, honor-him!

LETTER OF PAUL TO THE GALATIANS (4:4–7)

Happen time right, God send son, born from woman; understand, son himself follow law must. His duty what? Law remove. Finish, true become children his God can we. You true children God—proof what? Spirit same his son, God put-in-heart, spirit cry-out <u>Abba</u> [means Father]. You slave, no, push-aside; now son. Everything give-you, God want.

Word his Lord.

21

GOSPEL ACCLAMATION

Alleluia

Long-ago, God speak-to people how? Prophets.
Now God speak how? His son speak.

HOLY GOSPEL ACCORDING TO LUKE (2:16–21)

There Bethlehem shepherds hurry, find Mary and Joseph; there manger, baby. Succeed (pah!) understand recent inform-me about it baby. Shepherds out, inform++; #ALL listen, mouth-drop-open.

Mary see happen++, memorize, wonder-about. Shepherds go #BACK, glory give-to God, for-for? Everything they recent see, hear.

Eighth day, time circumcise, baby name-him Jesus—why? Long-ago, conceive~pregnant not-yet, angel tell Mary baby name Jesus.

Gospel his Lord.

Epiphany of the Lord

BOOK OF THE PROPHET ISAIAH (60:1–6)

Jerusalem, rise-up, shine! Glory from Lord shine-down-on you. See, earth dark, people obscure; but you, Lord shine-down, glory. Other countries people walk can because your bright-light; your radiance, kings they see. Look, they flock-to-you, your sons, daughters. You will see, inspire! Your heart flutter, overflow. Ocean, wonderful things pour-out-to-you. Other countries, their wealth bring-to-you. <u>Camels</u> line-up flock-to-you [from <u>Midian</u> and <u>Ephah</u>]; from <u>Sheba</u> they bring gold and sweet-whiff, announce praise Lord.

Word his Lord.

RESPONSORIAL PSALM (72:1–2, 7–8, 10–11, 12–13)

Lord, #ALL people here earth worship you.

King, please give-him wise judge / king son, give-him judge~fair
Your people, he control fair / your people poor, he mercy-them.

#ALL people he judge fair will / give peace forever
All-over earth king himself control / from here river to far area.

Kings theirs countries different++ / they bring-him, gold, various
#ALL kings honor-him / #ALL people serve him.

Person poor cry-out, he save-him / person weak, alone, he help
Humble, poor, he mercy-them / their life he save.

LETTER OF PAUL TO THE EPHESIANS (3:2–3, 5–6)

You know-that God finish give-me ministry for you. Secret plan God have, people long-ago know-nothing; but now apostles and prophets, Holy Spirit inform-them. His God plan what? United Christ Jesus, not~Jews, Jews, now same, member same body connect, same promise share through gospel preach.

Word his Lord.

GOSPEL ACCLAMATION

Alleluia

Star we see rise (sunrise)
We come for honor king.

HOLY GOSPEL ACCORDING TO MATTHEW (2:1–12)

Jesus born there Bethlehem during time-period King Herod reign. Now Jerusalem, star watchers from east arrive, question, "Where baby new king theirs Jews, where? Star rise we noticed, come here, honor want." King Herod disgruntled, Jerusalem people same. Religious leaders king summon, question where Messiah born. (Leaders) "Bethlehem [there Judea]. Long-ago prophet write, "Bethlehem true important town [in Judah]—why? it will born controller, himself lead my people Israel."

Star watchers Herod summon, question-them time star show-up, exact time what? Finish, tell-them, "Go, baby find. Learn whatever, come inform-me. Go honor-him, I want."

Three-of-them depart. Star follow (cl:1,3) until stop up-there, down-there house, baby there. Three-of them happy, enter, baby with mother Mary see, kneel, honor. Bring-box, take-off-lid, give-him gold, next-to-that sweet-whiff, next-to-that oil perfume.

Later, three-of-them sleep, dream, visualize, "Herod inform not." Close-vision, decide go home different way.

Gospel his Lord.

Baptism of the Lord

BOOK OF THE PROPHET ISAIAH (55:1–11)

Lord says, quote, Thirsty you? Come here water. Money have none? Come, eat; come, cost none, wine, milk drink. You money spend for things worthless, why? Satisfy nothing! Pay-attention me, eat delicious will you, live will you. Remember good things I promise <u>David</u>, I again promise you. Long-ago I cause <u>David</u> become leader for people, king over country; same-as Israel become leader—where? You don't-know. Other countries, now they don't-know you, they honor-you will, why? Lord your God give-you glory.

Search-for Lord now, possible find-him. Summon him now, he hear. Sinner, your life change. Ask Lord mercy, he willing forgive. Lord says, quote, "My thoughts, your thoughts, different. My tendency, your tendency, different. Heaven, earth separate (vertically), same my tendency, your tendency separate (vertically); my thoughts, your thoughts separate (vertically)."

Sky, rain, snow, earth wet, grow++ provide food and <u>seed</u> for farmer succeed, same God word speak-out, touch++, his want succeed.

Word his Lord.

or

BOOK OF THE PROPHET ISAIAH (42:1–4, 6–7)

Here my servant; I support-him, satisfy me. My spirit, I give-him. #ALL nations he judge fair will; quiet he, shout not. New grow, he walk, crush not. Cute candle, he "snuff" not. Establish judge~fair here earth will he; his teach #ALL people wait-for.

Myself Lord; I summon-you for help judge~fair succeed; I lead you, teach you, I establish you for relationship-with-God, you compare light for #ALL people. Blind, see will; prison, free; stuck dark, out.

Word his Lord.

RESPONSORIAL PSALM (Isaiah 12:2–3, 4bcd, 5–6)

God water you will drink, happy forever.

God himself save me / myself confident, afraid none
Lord give-me strong, brave / himself save-me.
God save you will / give you happy forever.

Thank-him Lord / praise his name
#ALL people, inform-them his actions / his wonderful name announce

Praise ASL-to Lord because he wonderful work / inform #ALL people
Jerusalem, sing happy / why? God himself there with you.

FIRST LETTER OF JOHN (5:1–9)

Suppose you believe Jesus himself true Christ, you child his God; you love Father, means you love any person himself connect-to-God. Suppose God his children we love, show how? Love God, his commandments obey. His commandments difficult, burden? No, God his children expert world defeat, how? Faith. Any person believe Jesus true Son his God, that-one finish world defeat succeed.

Jesus come through water and blood—not water alone, water and! blood. Spirit itself testify, prove. Have proof three: (1) spirit, (2) water, (3) blood. These three (on fingers) same, agree. We accept human testify—well, God, his testify worse! God testify what? Jesus his son, he prove.

Word his Lord.

or

ACTS OF THE APOSTLES (10:34–38)

Cornelius and people hordes his house, Peter preach-to them: quote, "Now I understand, oh-I-see, #ALL people God love equal, none prefer special. Any person from any country, he respect God and action right, God accept-him. That-one God inform people Israel, good #NEWS, peace, same Jesus Christ announce, himself Lord over #ALL. I think you finish know rumor, what? There Galilee Jesus immerse; later, Holy Spirit power God give-him. Jesus traveled-around, work good, cause heal, sin forgive; understand, God accompany."

Word his Lord.

GOSPEL ACCLAMATION

Alleluia

John look, see Jesus come (cl:1), said,
"Here Lamb of God, people sin he take-away."

HOLY GOSPEL ACCORDING TO MARK (1:7–11)

John Baptist preach what? Quote "Someone will come, himself important than me. His shoes I touch, not worthy enough, me. I immerse use water, but he will influence Holy Spirit." Happen Nazareth Jesus come (cl:1), arrive river, John immerse-him. Quick, sky open, Holy Spirit fly-down same compare bird. Voice from heaven they hear say, quote, "You true my cherished son. My favor touch, influence-you."

Lord himself king forever.

Gospel his Lord.

Ash Wednesday

BOOK OF THE PROPHET JOEL (2:12–18)

Lord says: "Come #BACK-to me; your heart give-me, with fasting, cry, grieve." Sin push-aside, come-to Lord your God. Himself full mercy, kindness, slow become angry, punish don't-want. Maybe mercy-us, bless us will he. Sacrifice give-to Lord your God. Blow-horn there <u>Zion</u>! Announce fasting; summon meeting; #ALL people assemble, (1) old people (2) children (3) babies assemble. Man, woman wedding near-future, suspend; priest cry, say, "Lord, save your people. Please punish us not; other countries oppress-us, they say 'Your God where?'"

Finish, Lord heart-soft; people, he mercy-them.

Word his Lord.

RESPONSORIAL PSALM (51:3–4, 5–6, 12–13, 14, 17)

Lord, we finish sin, please mercy-us

Mercy-me, God, yourself good / yourself heart-soft, my sin forgive
My guilt wash-clean / my sin please remove.

My sin I confess / my wrong I mind-dwell-on
Against you I finish sin / bad things I action, you see-me.

Heart clean give-me, God / spirit strong put-in-me
Reject-me not / your Holy Spirit take-from-me not.

Give me happy, save me / a spirit willing give-me
Lord, give-me sing / sign-ASL praise you will I.

SECOND LETTER OF PAUL TO THE CORINTHIANS (5:20—6:2)

We speak in-exchange Christ, means God speak through us. I beg you, yourself connect God. Jesus himself sin none, but God cause-him become full sin—for-for? Connect Jesus, we can become holy same-as God can we. God give-you grace, ignore not. God said, "Happen right time, I pay-attention you. Right day, I save you." Right time, now! Right day, now!

Word his Lord.

GOSPEL ACCLAMATION

Praise Lord Jesus Christ, king glory forever.

Heart clean give-me, Lord
Give-me happy, save me.

HOLY GOSPEL ACCORDING TO MATTHEW (6:1–6, 16–18)

Disciples, Jesus tell-them, "You religion actions—warning. Suppose other people see you, God praise-you not. Example, suppose money donate, don't announce, 'Hey, look at me! I donate' same hypocrite. They (people) praise, finish. Better secret donate, none know; God see, praise-you. Suppose you pray, don't stand pray voice loud, people look-up-and-down (cl:ff), yourself proud same hypocrite. Better pray secret, door closed, pray Father. God praise-you will. Suppose you fasting, don't expression frown, sad, hungry same hypocrite, people pity-them. Better you fasting, comb-hair, smile, people don't-know you fasting, but God knows. He praise-you will."

Gospel his Lord.

First Sunday of Lent

BOOK OF GENESIS (9:8–15)

<u>Noah</u> and son, God tell-them, "Now I establish promise~united you and your children future-generations, and #ALL living things: (1) bird, (2) animal various there <u>ark</u> with you boat. Promise what? #ALL living things, again flood destroy, never; earth, flood destroy, never. Happen I cause clouds over earth, rainbow notice, remember promise will I. Everything rain, flood destroy again, never."

Word his Lord.

RESPONSORIAL PSALM (25:4–5, 6–7, 8–9)

Lord, suppose your promise people cherish, you give-them love, honest.

Your want, please inform-me / your path, please show-me
Lead me way honest, teach-me / yourself God my Savior.

Lord, please remember your love / remember your mercy up-to-now
Yourself kind, please remember me / because yourself good.

Lord himself true~work good / sinners he leads right way
People humble, he lead right / his way he teach-them.

FIRST LETTER OF PETER (3:18–22)

Christ, himself good man, die for sinners—why? Lead-to God want. His body die, true, but his spirit live continue. His spirit finish go preach those spirits quote "prison." Who they? People live long-ago time-period <u>Noah</u>, they disobey during God patient wait <u>ark</u> boat build. Few people, altogether eight, boat-get-in, safe. Now you safe same, how? Baptize compare it boat. Baptize mean dirt (on-body) wash clean? No. Baptize mean our sin remove through Jesus die, resurrect, ascend heaven, now with God. #ALL angels and powers he control.

Word his Lord.

GOSPEL ACCLAMATION

Praise Lord Jesus Christ, king glory forever.

Bread alone give life not
God his little-story give life.

HOLY GOSPEL ACCORDING TO MARK (1:12–15)

Spirit send Jesus there land empty, stay 40 days — for-for? Devil tempt. Jesus, wild animals socialize. Angels serve him.

John Baptist arrest, jail, finish; Jesus show-up Galilee, annouce good #NEWS from God, quote: "God his promise near-future satisfied. God his kingdom (very) near. Your life change, good #NEWS believe."

Gospel his Lord.

Second Sunday of Lent

BOOK OF GENESIS (22:1–2, 9, 10–13, 15–18)

Abraham, God decide test. God call-out, "Abraham!" (Abraham) "What?" (God) "Your son Isaac, that-one you cherish, two-of-you go place name Moriah. Arrive finish, I show-you place you kill-him, sacrifice." Two-of-them travel, arrive, altar build, wood put-on-altar. Finish, Abraham son put-on-altar, draw-knife, ready stab. But angel call-out "Abraham!" (Abraham) "What?" (Angel) "Kill son not. Hurt not. I know-that you love God, why? Son sacrifice, you willing." Abraham look-around, notice sheep there, catch-it, replace-son, kill, sacrifice. Again angel call-out, say, "Lord inform-you, quote, 'Your son kill for me you willing, now I bless you excessively, you have descendants many! same star, same sand. Enemy, your descendants beat (shot-h), give bless for #ALL people—why? Because my command you obey.'"

Word his Lord.

RESPONSORIAL PSALM (116:10, 15, 16–17, 18–19)

Lord, two-of-us united during my life.

Faith have I, no-matter I complain, / "I awful suffer."
Suppose faithful person die / God see, cherish.

Lord, myself your servant, same my mother your servant / my slavery, you finish free
I kill~sacrifice for give-you thanks / I summon Lord help-me.

My promise, I keep / #ALL God people watch-me
Here Lord his house / here Jerusalem, middle, establish.

LETTER OF PAUL TO THE ROMANS (8:31–34)

Suppose God support-us, who possible defeat-us? God son, he (God) allow die for us. Give us more, he want. Who blame-us? God? No, he forgive us. Who punish us? God? or Jesus Christ, himself finish die, resurrect, now with God? No, he pray for us.

Word his Lord.

GOSPEL ACCLAMATION

Praise Lord Jesus Christ, king glory forever.

Cloud shiny, Father voice can hear, quote,
"He (hon) my cherish son. Pay-attention him."

HOLY GOSPEL ACCORDING TO MARK (9:2–10)

Jesus with Peter, James, John, four-of them group-go mountain. Jesus himself change. Clothes become white, wow. Elijah there, Moses there, three-of-them chat. Peter tell Jesus, "Tent three we build, for you++." He shocked, confused.

Wrong, cloud over. They hear voice say, "He (hon) my cherish son. Pay-attention him." Apostles look-around, see Jesus alone. Four-of-them group-go-down, Jesus strict tell-them recent happen announce not until Jesus die, resurrect finish. Three-of-them confidential, but they discuss what mean quote "die, resurrect"—puzzled.

Gospel his Lord.

Third Sunday of Lent

BOOK OF EXODUS (20:1–17)

God give commandment: "Myself Lord, your God; Egypt, there slave, I bring-you out free. Other <u>god</u> you honor? No! Statue bird, animal, fish, you make, bow-down, worship—No! Why? I myself jealous. Suppose father hate-me, sin, children his I punish, generations punish++. But suppose father love-me, my commandments obey, his children I mercy 1,000 generations mercy. Myself Lord your God, my name use bad way, not! My name use for curse, punish will I. Remember, seventh day holy. Six days you work++, #do++, but seventh day honor Lord your God. Who work can? None, not you, your son/daughter, your slave, your animal, other people live with you—none work. Six days Lord make heaven, earth, sea, everything; seventh day God rest. Seventh day, God bless, holy. Honor your mother~father, for-for? You have long life there land Lord God give-you. Kill not. Adultery not. Steal not. Lie about other people not. Drool your neighbor his house, wife, slave, animal want, not."

Word his Lord.

RESPONSORIAL PSALM (19:8, 9, 10, 11)

Lord, your little-story give-me life forever.

Lord his law perfect / soul inspire
Lord his command trust can / people know-nothing, give-them wise.

Lord his rule right / cause heart happy
Lord his command clear / easy understand.

Honor Lord give-you pure / continue forever
Lord his law true / #ALL (list down fingers) fair.

God his law important / than gold heap
Sweet than sugar / sweet than honey.

FIRST LETTER OF PAUL TO THE CORINTHIANS (1:22–25)

Jew people want proof, Greek people want wise, but we preach what? Christ crucify finish. Jew doubt, Greek puzzled; but for Christians, Jew, Greek, no-matter, Christ have power and wise same God. His quote "silly" true wise than people; his quote "weak" true strong than people.

Word his Lord.

GOSPEL ACCLAMATION

Praise Lord Jesus Christ, king glory forever.

People~world, God see, cherish, his Son he willing send
Any person believe~accept him (son), he live forever.

HOLY GOSPEL ACCORDING TO JOHN (2:13–25)

Jew Passover near-future, near; Jerusalem Jesus go-to. Temple arrive, people see, they #do-do? Cow, sheep, bird sell; other people sit, money budget share. Jesus make same whip, string, crack-whip, tables overturn, money coins roll-away. Jesus bawl-out, "Away! My Father house, you change sell place. Finish!" Apostles remember Bible predict, quote "Your house I enthused cherish"—oh-I-see. Jew people question, "Your authority action all-this, where? Proof where?" Jesus answer, "This (hon) temple destroy, 3 days later I set-up again." (Jews) "This temple build require 46 years, but you 3-days set up? Sick you!" True, Jesus mean what temple? His body. Later, Jesus die, resurrect finish, apostles remember, look-back Jesus story, oh-I-see, believe. Jesus stay Jerusalem for Passover. Many people connect—why? His action see, believe. But Jesus trust them not. Their tendency, he know. Explain-to-him about human nature, not~need; their heart he know.

Gospel his Lord.

Third Sunday of Lent, Year A

BOOK OF EXODUS (17:3–7)

People thirst water, disgruntled, tell Moses, "Egypt you force-me leave, for-for? Here water none, we die, our children, animals die." Moses pray-to-God, "#Do-do, me? Those people ready kill-me." Lord answer, "Go there with Israel leaders few, staff (cl:s,s) yours carry, there rock I stand. You staff-hit-rock, water flow-out, people drink can." Moses go, hit-rock, Israel people watch. That place name <u>Massah</u> and <u>Meribah</u>, why? There Israel people argue, wonder, "God here with us, <u>or</u> not, which?"

Word his Lord.

RESPONSORIAL PSALM (95:1–2, 6–7, 8–9)

Suppose today God inspire you feel, resist not.

Come, happy sing sign-ASL-to Lord / praise him our savior
Give-him thanks face-to-face / happy sing for him.

Come, bow-down, worship / kneel face-to-face Lord / himself made us
Himself our God / he cherish care-for us.

Suppose today God inspire you feel / resist not same long-ago
There desert your ancestors doubt / God work they see, no-matter, skeptical.

LETTER OF PAUL TO THE ROMANS (5:1–2, 5–8)

Now faith have, means we peace connect-to God with Jesus Christ. Faith Jesus give-us, now grace we receive can, and we boast, why? Glory his God we hope see. We hope . . . disappointed not. God his love inspire us, his Holy Spirit he-give-us. Past, time right, happen we weak sinners, Christ died for us. Suppose person true~work good, maybe friend brave willing die in-exchange, possible; but God prove love, how? We sinners, no-matter Christ died in-exchange.

Word his Lord.

GOSPEL ACCLAMATION

Praise Lord Jesus Christ, king glory forever.

Lord, #ALL people you save true,
Live~water give me, I thirst again never.

HOLY GOSPEL ACCORDING TO JOHN (4:5–42) (Shorter: omit text in brackets)

Town name <u>Samaria</u>, there near <u>Jacob</u> <u>well</u> (cl:circular, sides) Jesus arrive. Jesus tired, sit-down, time noon. Woman come (cl:1) for-for? Water draw-up. Jesus tell-her, "Water cup-give-me." Disciples finish go-out town, food buy. Woman say, "Myself woman <u>Samaritan</u>, you Jew, you ask-me for drink, why?" Understand, Jew, <u>Samaritan</u>, two-of-them get-along not. Jesus tell-her, "Suppose you know who I (hon), you will ask me for drink, and live water I give-you." (Woman) "You bucket none. <u>Well</u> deep. Water you draw-up how? This <u>well</u>, our ancestor <u>Jacob</u>, his family, drink, he give-us. You important beat-him (shot-h)?" (Jesus) "This water drink, thirst again will. My water drink, thirst again never. Water I give for live forever." (Woman) "Wow, your water give-me. Every-day come++ for water draw-up, bore me."

[(Jesus) "Go, husband bring-here." (Woman) "Husband none me." (Jesus) "Right—husband none you. You married five times, but man live with now, married not. You speak honest."]

(Woman) "Hey, yourself prophet. Hm. Our ancestor worship God here mountain, but Jew say worship there Jerusalem must." (Jesus) "Near-future, people worship God mountain, Jerusalem, no-matter. You worship, but you understand nothing. We understand—why? God save people through Jew generations. But near-future, true believer worship Father through Spirit and honest—those believers Father want worship him, why? Father himself spirit, means people worship-him want, themselves full Spirit and honest must."

Woman said, "I know-that Messiah will come, that-one name Christ, he will tell us everything." (Jesus) "That-one me (hon)."

[At-that-moment, apostles arrive, shock, why? Woman, Jesus chat-with. They question-to-him "Why? #Do-do?"—shhhh. Woman herself depart, town go-to, people tell, "Come, see man, he tell-me everything I action up-to-now—possible he Christ??" People curious, flock-to-him.

Jesus, apostles urge-him eat. Jesus tell-them, "I have food, you know-nothing." They puzzled, who bring-him food? Jesus inform-them, "My food what? Follow God his want, his work complete. You say, quote "Four months future, time harvest." Well, I inform-you, ready harvest now. Those people live forever, harvest them; finish, planter and harvester celebrate together. True, one person plant, other person harvest. You plant nothing, I send you for harvest. People previous work, preach finish—now you recruit succeed."]

Many people start believe Jesus because woman story, quote, "He tell-me everything I action up-to-now." Now people meet-him, invite-him stay. Jesus stay two-days. More people start believe, tell woman, "Past, your story we believe, but now myself finish see Jesus, know-that himself true~work savior for world."

Gospel his Lord.

Fourth Sunday of Lent

SECOND BOOK OF CHRONICLES (36:14–16, 19–23)

Judah, #ALL its prince, its priest and people, they sin++, worship false gods there Lord temple, that-one temple Lord finish bless there Jerusalem; they cause-it dirty. Often Lord God send-them informers—why? He pity-them, also his temple cherish. But informers from God they mock, warning ignore, prophet make-fun-of. Lord lose-temper. King there, God bring, clash, young men in temple kill++. He king kill men, women, young, old, weak, crippled, no-matter, kill #ALL. Temple his God, burn-down. Building #BURN, valuable things destroy. Anyone still alive, king force go-to Babylon, become servant for king continue until Persia succeed defeat, take control. These-things (on fingers) happen for-for? Well, Lord tell Jeremiah; true happen: "Rule seventh year none plant, these people obey not, now land settle, seventy years rest must." Later, happen Persia take control, first year, king name Cyrus, Lord influence-him announce, and write send-out, what? "Lord God there heaven, #ALL kingdoms he give-me, he tell-me build house for him Jerusalem, there Judah. Any you connect God people, go-to can, and I hope God accompany."

Word his Lord.

RESPONSORIAL PSALM (137:1–2, 3, 4–5, 6)

Suppose Jerusalem I forget, I shut-up forever should.

There country name Babylon, we sit, cry / remember, look-back Jerusalem
There (Babylon) trees tall, beautiful /
our harp (cl) we hang-up, abandon.

There our enemy question-us / our song, words what?
They encourage us feel happy / sing about Jerusalem.

We sing for Lord, how possible? / There far country, foreign, grief
Suppose Jerusalem I forget / my right hand paralyze should.

Suppose Jerusalem I forget / my tongue stick, talk can't
Jerusalem itself only / give-me happy.

LETTER OF PAUL TO THE EPHESIANS (2:4–10)

God whew! mercy; he love us so-much he give-us life connect Christ, no-matter we finish sin, die. He love you, save you. We connect Christ Jesus, God raise us, give-us place there heaven. Forever his love, kindness he show through Jesus. I tell-you again: God love you, save you because faith. Understand, self earn nothing. God give. You work++ save yourself? Impossible. Boast not. God, with Christ Jesus, two-of-them made us. He wants us live right, action good work he plan for us.

Word his Lord.

GOSPEL ACCLAMATION

Praise Lord Jesus Christ, king glory forever.

People~world, God see, cherish, his only son he give
#ALL people believe~accept Jesus, live forever.

HOLY GOSPEL ACCORDING TO JOHN (3:14–21)

<u>Nicodemus</u>, Jesus tell-him: "Moses snake (rh) stab (lh), raise-up (bh). Same must myself raise-up, crucified—why? #ALL those believe~accept, live forever will. People~world God see, cherish, his only son he give. #ALL people believe~accept Jesus, die not; live forever. God send his son for people criticize, punish? No! For save. Suppose you believe~accept him, save finish you. But suppose you believe~accept not, God punish. God judge how? Jesus light shine-on world, but people cherish dark than light—why? They bad actions. People actions bad, shine-on-me they hate, push away, their actions show, don't-want. But person he action honest, right, light shine-on-me he enjoy, show he action for God."

Gospel his Lord.

Fourth Sunday of Lent, Year A

FIRST BOOK OF SAMUEL (16:1, 6–7, 10–13)

<u>Samuel</u>, Lord tell-him, quote, "Oil pour-in-bottle, go-to <u>Jesse</u> there Bethlehem—why? His son I choose become king." <u>Samuel</u> see his (Jesse's) son name <u>Eliab</u>, think, "Wow, Lord choose-him." But Lord say, "You see-him tall, muscular, think thumbs-up, but I thumbs-down. People look-up-and-down (cl:f,f), think face~good, but God see his heart." Son seven <u>Jesse</u> bring, but <u>Samuel</u> tell-him, "God choose none. Other son have?" (Jesse) "Son young care-for sheep." (Samuel) "Summon-him. Sacrifice, feast suspend, wait he arrive." Son, <u>Jesse</u> summon-him. Himself face~nice, strong. Lord said, "That-one anoint." <u>Samuel</u>, oil anoint-him <u>David</u>; from-now-on God his spirit influence-him, inspire.

Word his Lord.

RESPONSORIAL PSALM (23:1–3a, 3b–4, 5, 6)

Lord, himself my care-er, give-me everything I need.

Lord, he my care-er, give-me everything I need / there grass area, he give me rest;
Near quiet river, he lead me; / my soul he inspire.

Right way he lead-me for his name honor
Suppose dark valley I walk (cl:1), / no-matter, afraid nothing.
He here with-me, accompany, full power, might / courage give-me.

Banquet he prepare, my enemies look-at-me / my head he anoint; my cup (lh) fill-up-overflow.
God good, kind, touch my life / die, I live there his home for ever and ever.

LETTER OF PAUL TO THE EPHESIANS (5:8–14)

Brother~sister, past, you dark, but now Lord give-you light. Live right, why? Light give things good, right, honest. Learn how satisfy Lord. Dark, bad actions, hands-off. Those actions bad, must you shine-on, show, become bright, good. Quote, "You sleep, wake-up. Dead, resurrect, live again. Christ give-you light."

Word his Lord.

GOSPEL ACCLAMATION

Praise Lord Jesus Christ, king glory forever.

Lord says, "Myself light for world.
Any person follow me, light for live I give-him."

HOLY GOSPEL ACCORDING TO JOHN (9:1–41) (Shorter: omit text in brackets)

Jesus walk (cl:1), notice man himself blind up-to-now, grow-up.

[Disciples question-to-him, "He blind, why? Himself sin, <u>or</u> his parents sin, which?" (Jesus) "None sin. He blind for God power show. God send me (hon) work during day light. Happen night, dark, work impossible. Myself light for world."]

Jesus spit-on-ground, mix, <u>mud</u> (mime smearing on man's eyes), finish, tell-him, "Go there <u>pool</u> name <u>Siloam</u>, wash-face." Man go, wash, #BACK, see can. People near~area habit see-him beg, said, "Man past sit beg, that-one he?" Some said yes, that-one he; other said no, face~same, but true different. Man himself say, "Yes, that-one me!"

[People question-to-him, "Now you see, how?" (Man) "Man name Jesus, <u>mud</u> he mix, my eyes smear-on, tell-me wash, now I see." (People) "Oh-I-see. Where Jesus, where?" (Man) "I don't-know."]

Now, people grab-him, put-him face-to-face Pharisee group. [That day, <u>Sabbath</u>, means work prohibit.] Pharisee question-to-man how possible see? Man again explain story. They said, "Jesus come from God not—why? He honor Sabbath not." But some said, "Suppose he sinner, wonderful work how?" Again man, they-question-to-him, "Jesus cause-you see—your opinion what?" (Man) "Prophet he."

[He blind up-to-now, now see can, Jews skeptical! Parents summon, question-to-them, "This your son? Himself true~work born blind? Now he see. How possible?" Two-of-them answer, "He our son, yes, blind up-to-now, yes, but how see, puzzled. Self question-to-him. He old enough, answer-you can he." Understand, parents fear Jews. Suppose two-of-them admit Jesus true Messiah, Jews kick-them-out. So, two-of-them answer, "Self question-to-him."

Again man summon, tell-him, "Glory give-to God. That Jesus, he sinner." Man answer, "He sinner, I don't-know. I know one thing. Past I blind, now I see." (Jews) "He #do-do? Cause-you see, how?" (Man) "Finish I tell you, again not~need. You up-to-now ignore-me—now become follower want?" (Jews) "You follow him, not me. We follow Moses. We know-that God talk-to Moses. God talk-to him? Skeptical!" (Man) (cl: between-the-eyes), "Oh-I-see, you skeptical, but he give-me see. We know-that suppose sinner pray, God ignore, but suppose good, holy person pray, God pay-attention. Other person cause blind become see, where? None! He from God, give-me see!"]

(Jews) "What? Yourself sinner up-to-now, you preach-to-us?" Grab-him, throw-him-out. Story~rumor Jesus hear, search, meet, said, "You believe son of man?" (Man) "I willing believe—where?" (Jesus) "You finish see. That-one me (hon)." (Man) "Yes, I believe." Kneel, worship.

[Jesus said, "I come-down-to (cl:1) world for-for? Judge. Those blind become see; those see become blind." Pharisee hear, question-to-him, "You mean we blind?" Jesus answer: "Suppose you true~work blind, none sin. But you say 'We see can,' means you sin have."]

Gospel his Lord.

Fifth Sunday of Lent

BOOK OF JEREMIAH (31:31–34)

Lord says, "Near-future, people Israel I promise~connect. Long-ago their ancestors (l) I promise~connect, that day Egypt, I lead-them out. They disconnect; show-them myself power must I. Now different. Now new promise~connect. My law, I put-in-them, their heart jot-down. Myself become their God; they become my people. From-now-on, friend, family they teach about Lord, not~need. #ALL know me will. Their wrong, I forgive. Their sin, I forget."

Word his Lord.

RESPONSORIAL PSALM (51:3–4, 12–13, 14–15)

God, heart clean please give-me.

Mercy-me, Lord, yourself good / yourself heart-soft, my wrong please forgive
My guilt remove / my sin forgive.

Heart clean please give-me, / spirit strong inspire-me
Please throw-me-out not / your holy spirit take-from-me not

Again cause-me happy, save-me / spirit enthusiastic give-me
Sinners, I teach-them your way / they connect-to-you will.

LETTER TO THE HEBREWS (5:7–9)

Time-period Jesus live here earth, he pray loud, cry, beg God save him, die not. God pay-attention him—why? He (Jesus) honor-him (God). He (Jesus) himself son, but obey he learn—how? Suffer. Succeed Jesus become perfect, #ALL people obey him he save.

Word his Lord.

GOSPEL ACCLAMATION

Praise Lord Jesus Christ, king glory forever.

Lord says, Serve me want? Follow me must.
Where I go, my servant follow.

HOLY GOSPEL ACCORDING TO JOHN (12:20–33)

<u>Passover</u>, Jerusalem many people swarm-to for worship. Have Greek few. <u>Philip</u> there, they ask-him, "Jesus we want see." He (Philip) inform <u>Andrew</u>; two-of-them go inform Jesus. Jesus say, "Now time for me (hon) glory. I inform-you, suppose ground <u>seed</u> fall not, die not, itself grow never. But, suppose itself die, grow will. Person life cherish, die he; but person life hate here world, live forever heaven will. Serve me want? Follow me. Where I go, my servant follow. You serve me, Father honor-you.

"My soul trouble, but pray God save me, refuse me. I come for die. Father, glory your name."

Heaven, voice say, "My name I finish glory; again glory will I." People hear, think thunder, but some say, "Angel talk." Jesus tell-them, "Recent voice benefit me? No, benefit you. Now world God judge. Now devil God defeat. I raise-up, #ALL people draw-to-me." Means Jesus die cross will.

Gospel his Lord.

Fifth Sunday of Lent, Year A

BOOK OF THE PROPHET EZEKIEL (37:12–14)

God says, quote, "My people, your grave, I open, raise-you live again, bring-you Israel, why? You know-that myself Lord, happen grave open, you rise, live again. My spirit, I give-you; your land, I put-you-on; finish, you know-that myself true~work Lord. I finish promise; true happen will."

Word his Lord.

RESPONSORIAL PSALM (130:1–2, 3–4, 5–6, 7–8)

Lord himself mercy-us, save us

Myself suffer, cry-out (to Lord) / my cry please pay-attention.
Lord, please, pay-attention / my sign-ASL, my prayers.

Suppose you, Lord, remember sin / who innocent, who?
But our sin you forgive / honor you, you want.

I trust Lord / his promise I believe
Guard wait for dawn / same Israel wait for Lord.

Lord himself mercy-us / save us he willing.
Israel he save / their sin forgive.

LETTER OF PAUL TO THE ROMANS (8:8–11)

Brother~sister, your body actions satisfy Lord can't (^). But you depend body not; you depend spirit, why? God his spirit live in you. Any person himself have none spirit, he connect God not-yet. But, suppose Christ live in you, your body sin, compare dead; but your spirit live still. Happen Jesus die, God raise-him live again. Suppose God spirit live in you, happen you die, God raise-you live again same.

GOSPEL ACCLAMATION

Praise Lord Jesus Christ, king glory forever.

Lord says, "Myself resurrect, live
Any person believe me, suppose he die, no-matter, live will."

HOLY GOSPEL ACCORDING TO JOHN (11:1–45) (Shorter: omit text in brackets)

[There town name <u>Bethany</u>, woman name <u>Mary</u>—that-one perfume pour, Jesus feet wash, hair dry-feet, that-one—with sister name <u>Martha</u>, their brother name <u>Lazarus</u>, he sick.]

<u>Lazarus</u>, his sisters, two-of-them send inform Jesus their brother sick. Jesus hear, say, "He die not. He sick for-for? Glory give God, my-turn glory me (hon)." Understand, three-of-them Jesus love, but two-days postpone. Succeed, he tell apostles, "Now <u>Judea</u> we go-to."

[Apostles argue, "Jew people kill-you want. Better not go." Jesus tell-them, "Day have twelve hours. Suppose person walk during day, fall-down not, why? Light. But suppose person walk during night, fall-down, why? Light have none. Our friend <u>Lazarus</u> now sleep, but I wake-him will." (Apostles) "Suppose he sleep, safe he." Know-that, Jesus mean die, but they think he mean normal sleep. Jesus tell-them straight, "<u>Lazarus</u> finish die. I happy, why? Now you believe will. Come-on." <u>Thomas</u> said, "Fine. Die with you accept."]

Arrive, Jesus find <u>Lazarus</u> bury four-days up-to-now. [That town, Jerusalem near, many people flock-to, pity <u>Mary</u> and <u>Martha</u> because brother die.] Jesus arrive, rumor <u>Martha</u> hear, go-to meet-him. <u>Mary</u> stay home. She (Martha) say, "Lord, suppose you here, my brother die not. Now, suppose you pray, God pay-attention." Jesus tell-her, "Your brother live again will." (Martha) "I know-that last day resurrect will." (Jesus) "I myself give resurrect, live; suppose person believe me, he die, no-matter, live will. You believe me??" (Martha) "Yes, Lord, now I believe yourself Christ, son of God, touch here world."

[Finish, she go-to sister <u>Mary</u>, tell her, "Jesus there want see you." <u>Mary</u> quick go (cl:1), meet—understand, Jesus touch city not-yet, stay-there, wait. There house, Jew friends see <u>Mary</u> go-out, they flock-after, guess~feel she go-to grave. <u>Mary</u> walk (cl:1), Jesus meet, kneel face-to-face-him, say, "Lord, suppose you come quick, my brother die not." She cry.]

Jesus look-at-her, heart~touch, himself become upset, said, "Body bury where?" Jew people say, "Come, see." Jesus cry. People say, "Wow, friend he cherish"—but some people say, "Blind, he cause-them see. Friend heal, why not?"

Jesus again upset, arrive grave, itself <u>cave</u> (cl), rock cover-entrance. Jesus say, "Rock push-aside." <u>Martha</u> tell-him, "Four-days up-to-now. Stink." (Jesus) "Finish I tell-you, suppose you believe, see God his glory will you." Stone push-aside. Jesus pray, "Father, I thank-you pay-attention-me. I know-that you always pay-attention-me, but now people see, believe you finish send-me here." Finish, Jesus cry-out loud, "<u>Lazarus</u>, come!" Wrong, man come (cl:1), wrap (like mummy, arms folded across chest, mime), face covered. Jesus said, "Unwrap him (mime), go-off."

Now Jews many see, believe.

Gospel his Lord.

Palm Sunday of the Lord's Passion

HOLY GOSPEL ACCORDING TO MARK (11:1–10)

Jerusalem, people swarm-to, Jesus tell disciples two, "Town ahead, go there, young donkey find, never person ride. Lead-to-here. Suppose someone ask you #do-do, tell-him, "Master need, but near-future give #BACK." Two-of-them go (cl:V), near gate find donkey young, untie. People few question, "#Do-do?" Answer same Jesus tell-them. "Oh-I-see, OK." Donkey, lead-to Jesus, coat throw-over-back, Jesus mount. Many people coat throw-on-ground, other people grass armful throw-down. People shout, "Hosanna! Bless him come (cl:1) name Lord! Bless future kingdom David. God there heaven save Jesus!"

Gospel his Lord.

or

HOLY GOSPEL ACCORDING TO JOHN (12:12–16)

There Jerusalem, time celebrate, people hordes hear rumor Jesus come. They #do-do? Palm leaf take-up, swarm-to, cry-out, "Hosanna! Honor him come (cl:1) name Lord! Himself true~work king its Israel!"

Donkey, Jesus find, sit~ride (sidesaddle), why? Long-ago write, quote, "Jerusalem, fear none. See, donkey, your king ride." Jesus his disciples see, puzzled; but later, Jesus glory they see, remember, oh-I-see. Bible long-ago write, true~happen.

Gospel his Lord.

BOOK OF THE PROPHET ISAIAH (50:4–7)

Lord God finish teach-me, give-me skill lecture; those people tired, I preach, cause-them excited. Every-morning, God help-me pay-attention-him, and I resist not, ignore not. People beat me,

I patient~accept; they pluck-beard mine, I offer more; they spit-on-me, I shield-face not. Lord God help-me, I embarrassed not. I stand-strong, know-that I ashamed not.

Word his Lord.

RESPONSORIAL PSALM (22:8–9, 17–18, 19–20, 23–24)

My God, you abandon-me — why?

People look-at-me, make-fun-of-me / they laugh, mock-me, say "Lord, he (man) depend-on / suppose God love him, save him will he."

Those people compare dogs / they surround-me (cl:4,4), drool
My hands, feet, they nail~hammer / my bones hurt, hurt, hurt.

My clothes, they share-around / for my coat, they roll-dice,
let's-see who win
God, please ignore-me not / hurry, help-me.

Your name I announce-to #ALL people / audience face-to-face,
I praise you
"Suppose you honor Lord, praise him / #ALL you Israel people,
glory give-him
Worship Lord, #ALL people."

LETTER OF PAUL TO THE PHILIPPIANS (2:6–11)

Attitude same Christ must you. Christ himself true~work God, but he cherish it (point upward) not. No, he humble born same slave, same us. Himself full human. He obey, accept cross die. Now, God raise him live again, give-him name #ALL other name exceed. Jesus name hear, every person kneel, there heaven, here earth, under earth, every voice announce, glory give God Father: Jesus Christ true Lord!

Word his Lord.

GOSPEL ACCLAMATION

Praise Lord Jesus Christ, king glory forever.

Christ himself obey Father, willing die there cross.
Now God raise-him-up, honor,
give-him name, #ALL other name exceed.

THE PASSION OF OUR LORD JESUS CHRIST
ACCORDING TO MARK (14:1—15:47)

Near Passover, Jew priest try figure how Jesus trick, arrest, kill. But during Passover, better not—why? Maybe people angry! There Bethany Jesus dinner with friend name Simon, happen woman enter, she have jar (cl) full perfume. She open, perfume pour-on Jesus. Few people say, "Waste perfume, for-for? Better sell, money get, give-to people poor."

Angry they. But Jesus tell-them: "Finish. You criticize-her, why? She right. People poor here always, money you give-them can. But I continue here not. Woman, she #do-do? My die, bury, she predict. I inform-you, future happen good #NEWS people announce, remember her, her action story will they."

Finish, apostle name Judas, he depart, priest~most go-to, plan Jesus hand-over. Priest~most excited, agree money pay-him. Right time hand-him-over, Judas wait-for.

Time Passover, habit lamb kill, eat; disciples two question-to Jesus, "Prepare Passover dinner, where?"

Jesus tell-them, "City, go-to, man meet, follow-him. House he enter, tell owner, 'Teacher need room for Passover dinner.' Room upstairs, large, nice he show you. That-one we eat there."

Two-of-them (cl:V) go-to city, everything happen same Jesus tell-them. Two-of-them prepare dinner. Dark, Jesus with apostles arrive room, sit-around-table, eat. Jesus tell-them, "I know-that one [of] you will betray me."

They heart-touch, #ALL said, "Not me."

Jesus tell-them, "One [of] you here. Understand, obey Bible plan must I. But that man betray-me, curse-him. Better he never born."

Finish, bread Jesus take-up, bless, tear-apart, give-out, said, "Eat; this my body."

Cup wine he take-up, thank (God), bless, give, #ALL drink. Jesus tell-them, "This my blood, mean new promise~connect. Blood I lose for many people save. Wine I drink again none until heaven I touch."

They sing praise, finish, walk group-go mountain Olives. Jesus tell-them, "Your faith doubt will. Bible says, 'Shepherd kill, sheep scatter.' But later, I resurrect, I meet-you there Galilee."

Peter said, "Maybe they doubt, but I doubt never."

Jesus tell-him, "I promise, tonight before rooster crows, deny me three times will you."

But Peter argue, "Die with you, I willing. Deny you never, me."

#ALL apostles said same.

Arrive place name Gethsemane, Jesus tell-them, "Stay here, I go pray." Jesus upset, afraid, tell-them, "My heart sad, ready die. Stay here, awake." He walk-away (cl:1), kneel, pray, "Father, you have power, everything you expert can. Please my suffer take-away. But your want, I accept."

Finish, Jesus come #BACK, find apostles asleep, said, "You sleep? One hour awake can't? Ready, pray none test you—why? Your spirit willing, but human nature weak."

Again Jesus go (cl:1) pray, same past. Again #BACK, they asleep. They sleepy, shrug. Third time Jesus go pray, #BACK, said, "Still asleep? Good~enough. Now time those awful men come, hand-me-over. Wake-up, come. See, my betrayer near."

Quick, Judas come forward (cl:1) with people hordes have sword, club (mime). Judas plan show-them who Jesus-–how? Tell-them, "That-one I hug, grab-him, throw jail."

He walk-to (cl:1) Jesus, said, "Rabbi," hug-him, They grab-him. One apostle sword-draw, slave, his ear cut-off. Jesus tell-them, "You come sword, club, for-for? Every-day there temple I teach, you arrest-me never. But now you follow Bible, arrest-me must."

They hear, afraid, un-popular. One young man they grab, clothes fall-off, naked escape.

Jesus, they lead-him face-to-face priest~most and other Jew leader few. Peter follow, priest~most area enter, find seat near fire, warm. Jew leaders question++ who story about Jesus prove he die must, but find none. Many people lie about Jesus, but their++ story conflict++. People few said, "We hear him say, this temple human hands make, he will tear-down, three-days later new temple set-up, human hands not make." But their++ story conflict++.

Priest~most question-to Jesus: "Those people story, you answer none?" Jesus quiet. Priest~most question-to-him: "Yourself Messiah, son of God?"

Jesus answer, "Yes. See me there heaven with God will you."

Priest-high said, "Witness we need none. You hear him lie. Decide what?"

They agree Jesus guilty, die must. Few [of] them spit-on Jesus; blindfold him, hit him, said, "Guess who hit-you."

Peter still there area, warm himself, servant girl notice-him, said, "You come with Jesus."

But he deny, "I (neg) understand you."

Wrong, rooster crow. Girl tell other people, "That man follow Jesus." Again Peter deny.

Later, other person said, "Yourself from Galilee; know Jesus must you."

Peter curse, "You talk, I know-nothing."

Again rooster crow; Peter remember Jesus predict, "Before rooster crow, deny me three times will you," gulp, cry.

Dawn, Jew leaders decide what #do-do. Jesus hands tie-up, lead face-to-face Pilate. He question-to Jesus, "Yourself king theirs Jews?"

Jesus said, "Yourself say that."

Jew leaders many accuse++. Pilate question-him again, "They accuse-you many. Answer what?" Surprise, Jesus answer nothing.

Every-year time Passover, Pilate habit one prisoner allow out free—who? People think-self. One prisoner name Barabbas, himself finish kill person. Pilate question-to people, "King yours Jews, you want out free?"

Understand, he know Jew leaders jealous, want Jesus die. Jew leaders tell people better ask for Barabbas out free. Pilate question-them, "Man named king theirs Jews, #do-do?"

People shout, "Crucify him."

Pilate question, "Why? What wrong?"

They worse shout, "Crucify him."

Pilate want them satisfied; Barabbas he allow out free; Jesus send for beat, finish, crucify. Soldiers lead Jesus large court room [name praetorium], Jew leaders hordes. Purple clothes they put-on-him same king, crown sharp++ put-on-head, bow++. "Honor king Jews!"

They spit, hit-him, kneel down false honor, mock-him. Finish, purple clothes take-off, his clothes put-on, lead-him for crucify. One man, named Simon, he work farm, they force-him cross help carry. Arrive Golgotha [name means Skull Place], wine they try give-him, pain reduce, but Jesus refuse. Crucify. His clothes share++, how? Roll-dice, let's-see who win. Time nine morning. Poster Jesus wrong what? Quote "King theirs Jews." Two other men crucified, right (cl:1), left (cl:1). People walk, look-up Jesus, said, "Ha-ha. Temple you destroy, build again three days. Save yourself, why~not? Cross come-down."

Other people said, "People few he finish save, but save himself can't. Suppose he true Messiah, king Israel—come-down now; we see, believe will."

Two men left, right (cl:1,1) same make-fun-of-him. Time noon, hit dark, continue all-afternoon. Jesus cry-out, "My God, you abandon me why?" People few hear, said, "He summon Elijah."

One person go, long-stick (cl:f,f), sponge (cl:something soft) stick-on-end, wine sour dip-in, hold-up-to-Jesus, said, "Now, let's-see Elijah come help-him."

Jesus cry-out, die.

(Kneel in silence)

Quick, temple curtain tear top-to-bottom. Soldier see Jesus die, said, "Clear, this man true~work son his God."

Women few over-there watch. Who they? Mary Magdalene and friends few, themselves since follow Jesus, his needs care-for. Also women several from Jerusalem there. Time sunset, tomorrow Sabbath. Man name Joseph [from Arimathea] arrive, himself Jew leader. He enthused kingdom God. He brave face-to-face Pilate, ask for Jesus body. Jesus die quick, Pilate surprised, question-to soldier Jesus finish true~work die? (Soldier answer) "Yes." (Pilate) "Oh-I-see." (to Joseph) "Go ahead."

Cloth Joseph bring, body take-down, cloth wrap-up, rock~grave (cl) body bring. Finish, rock (big) roll cover-entrance. Women watch, see body where.

Gospel his Lord.

Holy Thursday

BOOK OF EXODUS (12:1–8, 11–14)

There Egypt, <u>Moses</u>, <u>Aaron</u>, Lord tell-them, quote, "Now month must move-to-thumb, become first month [of] year. People Israel, inform-them what? From-now-on, this month tenth day must every family lamb take-up. Suppose it family small, share with other family can. Lamb itself must boy, age-one, perfect, wrong none. Can either sheep, goat, either. Reserve, four days wait; finish, time sunset #ALL people gather, lamb there++, kill++. Blood take home (cl:container); door post, lintel, blood paint-on. Same night, meat cook, eat with bread flat and <u>bitter herbs</u>. Eat how? Full clothes, shoes, staff (cl) hold, idea-same ready escape. Tonight happen <u>Passover</u> of Lord—why? Myself Lord, touch Egypt will I, every firstborn person and animal, I kill. Egypt people I judge, punish. But your house blood have (smeared-on). I see, pass. Egypt people I destroy, but touch you nothing. This day must you future remember, look-back, celebrate every-year forever."

Word his Lord.

RESPONSORIAL PSALM (116:12–13, 15–16bc, 17–18)

Our wine bless, itself become true blood his Christ.

Many good things Lord action for me / I pay-him how?
Cup holy wine, I drink will / Lord his name I summon.

Faithful follower die / Lord see, heart-touch
Myself your servant, same-as my mother / but you give-me free.

I sacrifice, thank-you / Lord his name I summon.
Lord I finish promise, succeed / #ALL people see can.

FIRST LETTER OF PAUL TO THE CORINTHIANS (11:23–26)

Lord inform-me, same I inform-you—what? Night before Jesus die, before, Jesus bread take-up, pray thank-God, break, said, "This true my body for you. You action this, remember, look-back me." Eat finish, Jesus wine take-up-cup, said, "This cup means new connect through my blood. Every time you drink, remember me." So, every time bread eat, wine drink, you announce Jesus die, until he comes again!

Word his Lord.

GOSPEL ACCLAMATION

Praise Lord Jesus Christ, king glory forever.

Lord says, "New order I give-you:
I up-to-now love you, same you love each-other must."

HOLY GOSPEL ACCORDING TO JOHN (13:1–15)

Time celebrate Passover, Jesus know near-future die, go-to Father. Jesus up-to-now always love his friends and continue love until last. Past, apostle name Judas, devil finish urge-him betray Jesus. Now, during eat, Jesus stand-up, coat-take-off. Understand, Jesus know himself come from God and near-future go #BACK God. Towel, Jesus tie-around-self, bowl, water pour-in; apostle feet wash, dry-with-towel. Take-turns-to Simon Peter. He said, "Lord, my feet you want wash??" (Jesus) "Now you understand none; later, understand clear." (Peter) "You wash my feet, nothing!" (Jesus) "Suppose I wash you not, two-of-us disconnect." (Peter) "Lord, please my feet and hands and head wash." Jesus tell-him, "Man finish bath, wash again not~need—only feet wash need. Himself finish clean, same you; but not #ALL." Jesus say not #ALL finish clean, why? He know who will betray-him. Wash finish, Jesus coat-put-on, sit-down, said, "?? You understand what I recent action for you? You name-me Teacher, Lord—right. I true~work Teacher, Lord. But your feet I wash. Mean what? You wash feet each-other must. I show-you example. Same-as-me serve must you."

Gospel his Lord.

GOOD FRIDAY

BOOK OF THE PROPHET ISAIAH (52:13—53:12)

See, my servant succeed will, raise-him-up, honor-him. Many people see-him, shock; his face ruin, not look-like true person. Many countries puzzle will, king mouth-drop-open. People they up-to-now never hear about God, they see, wonder. Who can believe what we finish hear? Who can understand Lord his plan? He (servant) grow-up face-to-face God compare young tree grow from ground dry. He look-like strong king not; we fascinate not. People hate, avoid him— true suffer he experience, pain used-to. People ignore-him, reject-him, honor not. But our weakness he accept, our pain he tolerate. We think God punish him, wrong. He willing accept punish for our sin in-exchange us. Beating he accept, now we healed; his pain heal us. Past, we compare sheep, think-self, wander (cl:1,1). We guilty, but our sin, God take-off-me, put-on-him. They beat-him awful, but he patient accept, complain none. He quiet, compare sheep~small lead, kill; or sheep~large stand (^^-legs), wait-for shear. They judge him, lead-away, kill, and who think more about him? Finish he die for sin theirs people, they bury him area with sinners—understand, himself wrong nothing, lie none. But God himself decide destroy him.

Suppose die for sin he willing, descendents many will he, and God his plan succeed will. Because he suffer, he future touch heaven. Through suffer, my servant cause many people connect God; their sin, their punishment he accept. So I honor-him, why? He patient accept die. People think himself sinner, but true sin theirs he remove, and God forgive them.

Word his Lord.

RESPONSORIAL PSALM (31:2, 6, 12–13, 15–16, 17, 25)

Father, my spirit I-give-to your control.

Lord, you I trust / allow me shame never
Yourself judge fair, save me / my spirit I-give-to your control.
Lord, yourself save me, / my faithful God.

My enemies mock-me / people laugh-at-me, friends un-popular
They see me walk (cl:1), escape / they forget me, feel myself compare same dead, worthless.

But I continue trust Lord / yourself my God
My life you control / my enemy persecute-me, you save me.

Please look-at-me, shine-on-me / yourself kind, save me
Hey, you people brave, stand-strong / #ALL you trust Lord.

LETTER TO THE HEBREWS (4:14–16; 5:7–9)

Our priest~most finish touch heaven—who? Jesus, son his God. Please continue faith. Our priest~most understand our weakness can, why? He experience tempt same-as-us, but sin never. Now we confident go (cl:1) face-to-face God, pray, know-that he mercy, love, help-me time I need help.

Past time-period during Jesus live here earth, he cry, pray God help-him, save life, die not. God pay-attention him—why? He (Jesus) honor him (God). Jesus himself God son, but learn how obey through suffer. Now he perfect; #ALL people they obey him, save them can he.

Word his Lord.

GOSPEL ACCLAMATION

Praise Lord Jesus Christ, king glory forever.

Christ himself obey, die there cross willing.
Now, God raise-him-up, honor,
give-him name, #ALL other name exceed.

PASSION OF OUR LORD JESUS CHRIST
ACCORDING TO JOHN
(18:1—19:42)

Jesus, with disciples, group-go Kidron Valley, garden there. That place Judas know, why? Jesus and disciples meet there often. Judas arrive with soldier and Jew leader few. They have lantern (cl), torch, sword. Jesus finish know what will happen, step forward (cl:1), said,

"You search-for who?"

(Jews) "Jesus from Nazareth."

"Myself (hon)."

Remember, Judas, he there. Happen Jesus say "Myself," #ALL step-back, fall-down. Again Jesus question-them,

"Want who?"

(Jews) "Jesus from Nazareth" (sign N-town).

"I finish tell-you, that me (hon). Let them go-out."

That happen for Jesus promise satisfy: People God give-me I lose one not-yet.

Simon Peter draw-sword; slave there, swing-sword, ear #OFF. [Slave, his name Malchus.] Jesus tell Peter,

"Put-in-sword. Obey Father plan, must I."

Soldiers and leaders arrest Jesus, hands tie, bring-him face-to-face Annas, himself father-in-law him Caiaphas, priest~most. That-one Caiaphas, past, he encourage Jews pick one man die for #ALL Jew people. Jesus (cl:1), Simon Peter with other disciple, two-of-them follow (cl:1, V). He, other disciple, priest~most know him, allow him enter, Peter left outside gate. Other disciple go-to woman there gate, chat, succeed open, "Come on!" Peter enter. Woman question-him,

(Woman) "You follower Jesus?"

(Peter) "Not me."

Night cold, servants, soldiers make fire, gather-around, warm rub-hands. Peter go-there (cl:1), warm rub-hands. Time~same, priest~most question Jesus about disciples, same-same about his teach. Jesus answer,

"I up-to-now preach open. I always teach there temple area, #ALL Jews gather, nothing secret. Question-me, why? Those people hear me preach, question-them. They know what I say."

Wrong, soldier slap-him (cl:1), slap-face, said,

"Priest~most, you rude-to-him, for-for?"

(Jesus) "Suppose I speak wrong, proof where? Suppose I speak honest, why slap-my-face, why?"

Finish, Annas send Jesus face-to-face priest~most name Caiaphas.

Time~same, Peter still warm rub-hands. People question-him,

(Woman) "You Jesus disciple?"

(Peter) "Not me."

One slave, himself cousin that-one ear cut-off, said,
"I finish see you with Jesus there garden."

Again Peter, "No!" Quick, rooster crow. Gulp.

Time sunrise, Jesus they-lead-him there court. Jew people themselves enter, shhh—why? Not pure. Suppose enter, Passover eat can't. Pilate (sign: P-government) come-out (cl:1), say,

"Accuse-him what?"

(Jews) "Law he break, we hand-to-you."

(Pilate) "Self judge him, follow your law, why-not?"

(Jews) "We kill person, prohibit."

Remember Jesus predict how will die? That-one.

Court Pilate again enter, question-him Jesus,
"?? Yourself king theirs Jews?"

(Jesus) "You, self interested, or other people inform-you about me, which?"

(Pilate) "Jew nothing me! Your people, your priest~most hand-you-to-me. Wrong #do-do you?"

(Jesus) "My kingdom here world not. Suppose my kingdom here, my people willing fight save me, allow hand-me-to Jews, refuse. But my kingdom not here."

(Pilate) "Oh-I-see. Mean you true~work king?"

(Jesus) "You name-me king. I born here world for-for? Teach honest. Any person himself honest cherish, my teach he pay-attention."

(Pilate) "Honest! What mean honest?"

Finish, Pilate again come-out (cl:1), announce Jew hordes,
"My opinion, that man innocent. Remember your tradition: every-year, time Passover, one prisoner I allow out free. ?? You want king theirs Jews out free?"

(Jews) "We want Barabbas out free, not Jesus."

Who Barabbas? Rebel.

Now, Pilate send Jesus for beat. Soldiers make sharp++ twist-around, crown-on-head, thorns-dig-in. Purple coat, put-on-him. One-by-one (cl: 1,1) approach-him, slap++, say,
"#ALL honor king theirs Jews!"

Again Pilate come-out (cl:1), tell people,
"Pay-attention-me! Jesus bring here, you look-at-him, see he innocent will you."

Jesus come-out (cl:1) crown~thorns, coat purple.
(Pilate) "There (hon)."

Quick, people see-him, shout,
(Jews) "Crucify him!"

(Pilate) "Selves crucify him. None reason have I."

(Jews) "We have law require he die, why? He name himself God Son."

Pilate hear, afraid. Again court enter, question-him Jesus,
"From where, you?"

Jesus answer none.

(Pilate) "You speak refuse? You know-that I have power, can allow out free, crucify you, think myself?"

(Jesus) "You have power because God give-you. You sin, but person he betray-me, his sin worse."

Now Pilate enthusiastic Jesus out free, but Jews more shout,
"Suppose you allow Jesus out free, means Caesar you support not. Any person name himself king, he enemy Caesar."

Their little-story, Pilate hear, oh-I-see. Jesus bring. Sit judge chair, that place name Stone Pavement [Jew word, Gabbatha]. Understand, that day Jew people must prepare for Passover. Now time noon.

Pilate tell-them,
"Your king, there (hon)."

(Jews) "Away! Crucify him!"
(Pilate) "What! Crucify your king?"
(Jews) "Our king Caesar."

Pilate gulp, hand-him-over. They lead Jesus, himself cross carry-on-shoulder; arrive place name Place of [the] Skull [Jew word, Golgotha], crucify him with other men two, right, left (cl:1,1), Jesus middle. Pilate write poster put-over-head (cl) "Jesus from Nazareth, King theirs Jews," language three (1) Jew, (2) Latin, (3) Greek. Many people read poster. Understand, that place, city, near. Jew priest tell-him Pilate, (Jew) "Hey, better jot-down 'That man name himself king theirs Jews.'"

(Pilate) "I finish write, period."

Jesus crucify finish, his clothes, soldiers share++. Left one coat—#do-do? Tear, don't-want. Decide roll-dice, let's-see who win. Reason? Satisfy Bible verse, "My clothes, they share-around, for my coat they roll-dice."

Near cross, there group, who? Jesus his mother, her sister, other friend, and Mary Magdalene. Jesus see mother with disciple best-friend, tell-her,

"Woman, there your son."
Next-to-her disciple,
"There your mother."

From-then-on, he disciple care-for Mary.

Jesus know-that his duty completed, said,
"I thirst."

There jar full cheap wine. Soldier (mime long, skinny reed, soft-thing put-on-end, dip in jar, hold up to Jesus). Jesus taste, said,
"Now complete, finish."

Head-bow (cl:s) die.

(Kneel in silence)

That day Passover meal Jews prepare must, body (point one, two, three) leave-there cross, don't-want, why? Special holy day. They ask Pilate please their legs break, hurry die, body take-down, carry away. So, soldiers go, man there (r), there (l), swing-club-right, swing-left; but Jesus himself finish die, swing-club not~need. One soldier draw-sword, stab-him; wrong, blood, water, flow-down. One witness see happen, he inform for help-you believe. Bible predict finish satisfy, "His bone, break none." Other verse, "Person they finish stab, they look-at (cl:4,4)."

Later, man name Joseph [from Arimathea], himself secret follower, he ask Pilate, "Don't-mind body I take-down?" (Pilate) "Go ahead." (Joseph) "Thank you." Take-down-body. Other secret follower, name Nicodemus, he bring oil and spice, container (cl) 100 pounds. Jesus body, wrap++, oil wrap++, follow Jew habit bury. Cross there, almost-nothing there garden, it have new tomb, body put-in-tomb not-yet. Time++, hurry, Jesus body put-in-tomb, leave-there, why? Must dash home, prepare for Passover.

Gospel his Lord.

Easter Vigil

FIRST READING: BOOK OF GENESIS (1:1—2:2)

Before heaven, earth set-up, before, have dark, wind, water messed-up. God said, "Give light!" God see, like, decide light, dark separate, name-it (r) day, name-it (l) night. First day, finish. Now God say, "Water separate (top, bottom) must." Make dome (cl), water above, name sky. Second day, finish. God said, "Water push-together, dry land area." Land name earth, water name ocean. God see, satisfied. Decide grow flower, tree, fruit, various. Pah! Grow++. God like. Third day, finish. Now God say, "Sky need lights during day, night, for-for? Count day, month, year." So, God make sun bright-light for day, moon, stars small light for night. God look-around, satisfied. Fourth day, finish. God think, say, "Animals, where? Fish, bird, earth need." God make animals various, there ocean fish, there sky fly. God bless-them, tell-them go-ahead all-over earth spread. Fifth day, finish. Now God say, "Earth need animals more, cow, insect, various." Pah, animal <u>wild</u>, cow, insect, snake, various. God happy. Last, God say, "Now man we make, same-as us. Fish, animal, bird, man control will." So, man, woman, God make. He bless-them, tell-them go-ahead, earth spread-out, take-up control. Plus, God give-them tree, fruit, #VEG various for eat; #ALL animals, they grass, plant eat. Sixth day, finish. Heaven, earth, God work six days, make++, finish, seventh day, God #do-do? Rest.

Word his Lord.

RESPONSORIAL PSALM (Psalm 104:1–2, 5–6, 10, 12, 13–14, 20, 35)

Lord, your spirit send-down, all-over earth become new.

My soul bless Lord / God himself wonderful true
Yourself full power, glory / clothes shine-out-bright

Earth, yourself make, establish / stand-strong forever
Oceans you group-left, group-right / mountains you set-up.

Rivers you send flow / mountains, flow-around
There, birds live / their song speak-upward-to heaven.

There heaven, you give rain / earth food grow, grow
Grass for animals eat, grow ++ for people / bread make, eat.

Your many actions true wonderful / you wise, make++
All-over earth, you make++ / my soul praise Lord.

or (Psalm 33:4–5, 6–7, 12–13, 20–22)

All-over earth show Lord himself good.

Lord his word appropriate / his action honest
Judge~fair, good action, he love / his kindness touch all-over earth.

Lord himself finish heaven make / angels, he invent, cause
Here earth, water he group-left / ocean group-right.

That country honor Lord, God bless them / he choose them, cherish
Heaven, Lord look-down / #ALL people he see.

We patient wait-for Lord / himself help-us, protect us
Lord, please mercy-us / we depend-on you alone.

SECOND READING: BOOK OF GENESIS (22:1–18)

Abraham God test. God call-out, "Abraham!" (Abraham) "What?" (God) "Your son Isaac, that-one you cherish, two-of-you go place name Moriah. Arrive finish, I show-you where you kill, sacrifice." Tomorrow morning, donkey put-on-saddle, son, two-of-them with servants two, wood carry, start travel. Third day, Abraham see there place, tell servants stay here, two-of-us go, worship, #BACK. Wood, son back, put on; walk (cl:1,1) "Father?" (Abraham)"What?" (Son) "Animal for sacrifice, where?" Gulp. (Abraham) "God give will."

Two-of-them travel, arrive, altar build, wood put-on-altar. Finish, Abraham son put-on-altar, draw-knife, ready stab. But angel call-out "Abraham!" (Abraham) "What?" (Angel) "Kill son not. Hurt not. I know-that you love God, why? Son you willing sacrifice." Abraham look-around, notice sheep there, catch-it, replace-son, kill, sacrifice. [That place, Abraham name-it <u>Yahweh-yireh</u>, means, "Lord will see."] Again angel call-out, say, "Lord inform-you, quote, 'You willing your son kill for me, now I bless you excessively, you have descendants many! same star, same <u>sand</u>. Enemy, your descendants beat (shot-h), give bless for #ALL people—why? Because my order you obey.'"

RESPONSORIAL PSALM (Psalm 16:5, 8, 9–10, 11)

Lord, I trust only-you.

Lord, I cherish-you / my future, you lead, protect
Lord I follow always / God accompany, I afraid nothing.

My heart happy, my soul celebrate / my body "laid-back," confident
I know-that my soul God abandon never / my body he care-for, ruin never.

Way [to] heaven, you show-me / happy with you, will I
Enjoy socialize together / forever, ever.

THIRD READING: BOOK OF EXODUS (14:15—15:1)

Moses, Lord tell-him, "You complain, for-for? Israel people, tell-them go straight-ahead. Your <u>staff</u> (cl) hold-out, ocean separate will, dry area, people flock-through. Egypt soldiers arrogant, follow, but my glory see will they. Know myself true~work Lord will they.

God, his angel up-to-now lead, now behind, protect. Plus, cloud past front, now behind, obscure. Dark, Egypt people, Israel people look-at-each-other, see none. Moses hold-staff-out, wrong, east wind blow all-night, morning see water separated, dry area (middle).

Israel people flock-through, safe, water left, right. Egypt soldiers follow, horse, wagon flock-through. But Lord give-them afraid, they hurry, stuck <u>mud</u>, wrong, decide back-up, Israel defeat-them don't-want.

But Moses, God tell-him, "Again hold-staff-out, water close will." Moses hold-staff-out, water flow-together, Egypt soldiers stuck, escape can't, #ALL die. Israel people recent walk there dry, water left, right. God save. Israel look, Egypt soldiers dead see, whew! Lord power! They afraid, Lord and Moses they believe. They sing, praise Lord, quote: "I sign-ASL-to Lord, he wonderful succeed; horse, soldier he throw-into ocean, drown."

RESPONSORIAL PSALM (Exodus 15:1–2, 3–4, 5–6, 17–18)

We sing sign-ASL-to Lord; himself full glory.

I sign-ASL-to Lord, himself glory win / horse, "wheelchair~reins," he toss-into ocean
Lord himself give-me strong, brave / he finish save me
Himself my God, praise him / my God up-to-now, I worship him.

Lord himself compare soldier / his name quote, <u>LORD</u>!
Egypt king, his "wheelchair~reins" God toss-into ocean /
his expert soldiers, water drown.

Soldiers, water rise, cover-head / they compare same rock, drown-fast Lord, you power action it (point to drowned soldiers) / enemy, you destroy.

But your people, you save / there mountain, you establish home
That place, you decide stay, control / that holy place yourself choose
Lord control forever, ever.

FOURTH READING: BOOK OF THE PROPHET ISAIAH (54:5–14)

Your quote "husband," who? Lord himself, he finish make you. Himself save you. He summon-you, compare young wife, her husband abandon-her, now summon-her #BACK. God says, "Short time, I abandon-you, but now heart-soft, I accept you, love you. Short time, I angry, ignore-you, but now cherish you. Remember time-period Noah, I promise earth flood destroy again never? Now I promise angry again never. Suppose mountain collapse, no-matter, I love you continue." Lord himself mercy-you, peace give-you. Pity those people; they troubled, worried. Your city God build new, foundation sapphires, walls precious (cherish) rock-shiny. Your tower (cl) he make ruby red sparkle, your gates and walls, diamonds. Your son, Lord himself teach-them; your children peace will. You, God establish, fear none, oppression none, destroy none.

Word his Lord.

RESPONSORIAL PSALM (Psalm 30:2, 4, 5–6, 11–12)

Lord, I praise you, why? You finish save me.

Lord, I praise you, why? You finish save me /
my enemy beat-me (shot-h), you prohibit
Die, you save me / people go-to hell, you grab-me-out.

You faithful people, sing praise Lord / thank-you his holy name
He angry short / but he mercy forever
Time night, cry / but sunrise, celebrate~happy.

Lord, please pay-attention-me, mercy-me / Lord, please help-me
Past, I heart-wring, now you give-me dance / I thank-you forever.

FIFTH READING: BOOK OF THE PROPHET ISAIAH (55:1–11)

Thirsty you-all? Come-here, water. Money none? Come-here, food have. Come, pay none, cost none. Wine, milk drink. Money spend for things can't eat, why? Satisfy not. Pay-attention-me, eat good, enjoy. Come-here me (hon), pay-attention-me, live will you. I again promise connect-to-you, same long-ago I promise united <u>David</u>. Remember <u>David</u>, my power he prove, how? Country different++, he defeat. Same will you. Country you don't-know, you summon; they don't-know you, no matter, come quick, obey. Why? Lord give-you power, glory.

Search-for Lord now, why? Possible find him. Call-to-him now, why? He near. Sinner, life~change must. Sin thought, push-aside. Look-at Lord, ask mercy-me; God forgive always. Lord says, "My thought, your thought, same not. My way, your way, different. Know-that heaven high, earth f-a-a-a-r separate? That compare my way, your way separate; my thought, your thought separate." Know-that heaven water sprinkle-down soil, wet, cause grow++, finish, water rise-up, dissolve. Grow++ make #seed for farmer, plus grind-up, make bread for people eat. Same compare my word speak~outward, action++ what I want; finish, #BACK succeed.

Word his Lord.

RESPONSORIAL PSALM (Isaiah 12:2–3, 4, 5–6)

Happy, celebrate will you, why? God finish save you.

God finish save me / now I afraid nothing.
Lord give-me brave, strong / himself true~work my savior.
Happy, celebrate will you / God finish save you.

Thank-you Lord / his name praise
#ALL people inform-them his actions / his holy name announce.

Sing praise Lord his wonderful succeed / all-over earth inform.
Jerusalem people, shout happy! / Holy God finish touch Israel.

SIXTH READING: BOOK OF THE PROPHET BARUCH (3:9–15, 32—4:4)

Israel people, pay attention. Commandments give-you live. ?? How happen, here foreign country you live, enemy you socialize? God his wise, you ignore, why? Suppose you up-to-now obey God, peace will you. You become smart, strong, understand++, same-same have long live, light, peace, will you. Who finish succeed wise? Who finish study, understand?

Only God himself true~work wise. God know everything. Earth, he set-up; animal he make++; sunset, sunrise, he order; stars he put++; he summon-them, they happy answer, "We here!" Who compare equal our God, who? None. Everything he understand, Jacob and Israel people he teach.

Now here earth have wise. Wise find where? There book God his Law. Suppose law follow, live; but law ignore, die will. Come, law accept, itself give-you light for live. Honor other god not, follow other religion not. We lucky, why? Satisfy God want, we know how.

Word his Lord.

RESPONSORIAL PSALM (Psalm 19:8, 9, 10, 11)

Lord, your little-story give-me life forever.

Lord his law perfect / our soul inspire
Lord his decide, trust can / people humble become wise.

Lord his commandment right / cause heart happy
Lord his order clear / we understand can.

Honor Lord true / continue forever, ever;
Lord his law true / #ALL (down fingers) fair.

God law (l), gold heap (r) / worth, which? It (l, law).
Honey sweet, delicious / same his law sweet.

SEVENTH READING: BOOK OF THE PROPHET EZEKIEL (36:16–17a, 18–28)

Lord inform-me, quote, "Israel people, their action awful sin. Angry me, why? They kill++, plus idol worship. I force-them scatter country different++. They arrive, embarrass me; those people know-that my people, I force-them scatter. My holy name, those people make-fun-of; now, mind~change me, heart~soft, my people come #BACK I allow. Tell Israel people, quote 'You come #BACK I allow why? Because I cherish you? No. My holy name I support. You embarrass me, now prove my name true holy will I. Those countries, they know I true holy will they, how? Prove will I. Israel people I gather, #ALL country I gather, bring-you here home. Clean water I wash-you, dirt remove, your idols destroy will I. Heart new, spirit new I give you—old heart hard I remove, new heart exchange. My spirit I give-you, my law you follow will. Here land you live forever; you become my people, I become your God.'"

Word his Lord.

RESPONSORIAL PSALM (Psalm 42:3, 5; 43:3–4)

(Option A: when Baptism is celebrated)

Deer thirst water, same compare my soul thirst God.

My soul thirst-for God / I go-to-him, his face see, when?

Group, I join-in / group-go there temple
We happy, shout thank-you / people hordes celebrate.

Lord, your light, faithfulness, give-me / lead me
Your holy mountain I arrive / your home enter.

God his altar I go-to (cl:1) / he give-me happy, satisfied
Finish, I sing thank-you / God, my God.

(Option B: when Baptism is not celebrated)   (Isaiah 12:2–3, 4, 5–6)
(found after the fifth reading)

(Option C: when Baptism is not celebrated)   (Psalm 51:12–13, 14–15, 18–19)

Lord, heart clean, holy, give-me.

God, please heart clean give-me / spirit strong inspire me
Please reject-me not / your Holy Spirit take-out-of-me not.

Give-me happy, save me / a spirit willing give-me
Sinners, I teach-them your way / they connect-to-God will.

Sacrifice, you enjoy not / suppose animal I kill, burn-up, you thumbs-down
My spirit humble I sacrifice / heart humble, sorry, you accept.

LETTER OF PAUL TO THE ROMANS   (6:3–11)

Brother~sister, we baptized, show we connect Christ Jesus. We finish die same-as-him. During baptize, we die, bury with Jesus, same-as-him. Jesus, Father raise-up live again, same new life he give us. Suppose we die connect Christ, resurrect connect-him will. We know-that our old sinner body finish die with Jesus there cross; means we fascinate, habit sin, finish. Suppose man die, he sin again can't. Suppose we die with Christ, we believe live again with him will. We know-that Jesus once die, resurrect, finish; again die never. Die, it defeat-him not. He die once for sin destroy; now he lives for God. Same must you think yourselves dead for sin, live for God.

Word his Lord.

GOSPEL ACCLAMATION   (Psalm 118:1–2, 16–17, 22–23)

Alleluia, alleluia, alleluia!

Thank-you Lord, himself good / his mercy continue forever.
People there Israel say quote, / "His mercy continue forever."

Lord himself action mighty / Lord his strong we honor.
I die never, live will I / Lord his action I announce.

Stone people reject / now itself most important support.
God his plan now satisfy / we see, wow, wonderful!

HOLY GOSPEL ACCORDING TO MARK   (16:1–7)

Sabbath finish, Sunday early-morning, sunrise, women three [(1) Mary Magdalene, (2) other Mary, (3) Salome], three-of-them decide go-to grave. Three-of-them concerned, why? It grave have rock big (cl:c,c), heavy; wonder who roll-it-aside, who? Arrive, see rock ready roll-aside, finish.

Grave enter, see young man sit (r), clothes white! Shock they. He tell-them, "Shock not. You search-for Jesus, that-one recent crucify. Not here. Body past here, now gone. Three-of-you go, inform disciples, Jesus finish go-to Galilee; see-him there will, same Jesus promise."

Gospel his Lord.

Easter Sunday

ACTS OF THE APOSTLES (10:34, 37–43)

<u>Peter</u> tell people, "You finish know story rumor about Jesus, start there <u>Galilee</u> baptism, Holy Spirit and power God give-him. Jesus travel-around, good work++; those people have devil influence-them, heal. God accompany-him. We finish see Jesus #do-do there Jerusalem. Last, Jews kill him, crucify. But third day God raise-him live again, people see-him—but not #ALL. God choose witness few, who? We apostles. Jesus die, resurrect finish, we eat with him. He order us preach #ALL people—preach what? God choose Jesus for judge #ALL people, alive, dead, both. Up-to-now prophets preach about Jesus: suppose you believe him, your sin God forgive."

Word his Lord.

RESPONSORIAL PSALM (118:1–2, 16–17, 22–23)

Today Lord make special, we happy celebrate.

Thank-you Lord, himself good, / his mercy continue forever
People there Israel say quote, / "His mercy continue forever."

Lord himself action mighty / Lord his strong we honor
I die not, live will I / work his Lord I announce.

Rock, that-one people reject / itself now most important support
Lord his plan now satisfy / we see, wow, true wonderful.

LETTER OF PAUL TO THE COLOSSIANS (3:1–4)

You finish resurrect with Christ. Now, focus heaven things, there Christ with God. Cherish things connect heaven more-than things connect earth. Die finish you! Your life now secret hide with Christ and God. Happen Christ show-up, you with him full glory will.

Word his Lord.

or

FIRST LETTER OF PAUL TO THE CORINTHIANS (5:6b–8)

You know yeast? Bread make, yeast put-in, knead (mime), increase-in-size. Now, old yeast throw-out, make bread new, clean. Christ finish sacrifice himself. Now we celebrate, old bread compare sin, throw-out; new bread compare honest, celebrate.

Word his Lord.

GOSPEL ACCLAMATION

Alleluia

Christ, himself our Lamb, kill~sacrifice
Now we celebrate with Lord.

HOLY GOSPEL ACCORDING TO JOHN (20:1–9)

Early-morning first day week, still dark, Mary Magdalene arrive grave, see rock roll-away, gulp; run tell Simon Peter and other disciple, that-one best-friend Jesus, "Lord body, someone steal, put where, I don't-know." Two-of-them (cl:V) go-to grave. Second, he run, arrive first. Enter, shhh. Look-in, see cloth wrap left ground. Peter arrive, enter, see cloth there ground, other cloth wrap-around head, separate, left-there. Now second disciple enter, see, believe! Remember, predict about Jesus die, resurrect, two-of-them understand not-yet.

Gospel his Lord.

Second Sunday of Easter DIVINE MERCY SUNDAY

ACTS OF THE APOSTLES (4:32–35)

Believers group, they heart united, mind united. None selfish "Mine, not yours"; everything share++ equal. Apostles power(ful) preach about Jesus resurrect. People respect-them. None hungry, poor, why? Every person house, property have—sell, money receive, give-to apostles for share, give++ what they (people) need.

Word his Lord.

RESPONSORIAL PSALM (118:2–4, 13–15, 22–24)

Thank-you Lord, himself good, his love continue forever.

People Israel say, / "God mercy continue forever."
Priest #ALL say, / "God mercy continue forever."
People honor Lord say, / "God mercy continue forever."

Myself struggle, frustrate++, / but Lord help-me.
Strong, brave, Lord give-me / he save me.
Happy announce he succeed / inform those people good.

Rock, that-one people since reject / now most important support.
Lord himself cause happen / we see, wow, wonderful.
Now day Lord make special / we happy, celebrate.

FIRST LETTER OF JOHN (5:1–6)

Suppose you believe Jesus true Christ, you child his God. Suppose man you love, means his child you love same. Love God children, you want? Well, love God, his commandment obey. Love God means his commandment we obey can, difficult not. #ALL God children, they finish world evil defeat—how? Power what? Our faith. Who can defeat world, who? That person believe Jesus true son his God. Jesus come (cl:1) through water and blood—not water only, water and blood both. Holy Spirit witness honest.

Word his Lord.

GOSPEL ACCLAMATION

Alleluia

Lord says, You believe me, reason? You finish see.
Bless those people see me not-yet, still believe.

HOLY GOSPEL ACCORDING TO JOHN (20:19–31)

First day [of] week, night, disciples assemble room, close-door, lock, why? Afraid Jew leaders. Wrong, Jesus show-up, said, "Peace I give-you." Finish, hands, feet, side Jesus show. Disciples excited, happy. (Jesus) "Peace I give-you. Father finish send me; now my-turn I send you." Jesus inhale, spread-out-from-mouth, said, "Holy Spirit give-you. Suppose sin you forgive, sin dissolve. Suppose you forgive refuse, sin stay." One apostle name Thomas [that name means twin], he not there. Other disciples inform-him, "We finish see Lord!" He skeptical! "Happen I myself touch Jesus, his hands (point to nail marks), his side slit-open, touch-it, believe will I." Next-week, again disciples assemble room, also Thomas with, door locked. Jesus show-up, said, "Peace." Look around, there Thomas, tell-him, "Come-here (crook finger). My hands touch; side, touch. Skeptical, push-aside; now believe!" (Thomas) "My Lord, my God." (Jesus) "You believe now because you see me. Bless those people they see me not-yet but still believe." Jesus action many wonderful work, #ALL jot-down shhh, but disciples see. Recent few (on fingers) jot-down for-for? help-you believe Jesus true Messiah, Son his God. You faith have, live forever will.

Gospel his Lord.

Third Sunday of Easter

ACTS OF THE APOSTLES (3:13–15, 17–19)

<u>Peter</u> tell people: "Our ancestor Abraham, [<u>Isaac</u>, <u>Jacob</u>] God control; same God finish glory give-to Jesus—that-one you hand-over [to] <u>Pilate</u> for crucify. Jesus, Pilate willing allow out free, but you prefer killer out free. Jesus give you life; you kill-him. But God raise-him live again. Ourselves finish see, prove.

"I know-that these-things (on fingers) you action, know-nothing. Your action, God use for his plan satisfy, same he long-ago inform prophets—what plan? Messiah suffer, die must. Now, your life change~improve. Accept God; your sin he forgive."

Word his Lord.

RESPONSORIAL PSALM (4:2, 4, 7–8, 9)

Lord, please your face shine-on-me.

I call-out, God please answer-me / during time-period struggle, you help-me
Please mercy-me / my prayer, pay-attention

Know-that Lord action wonderful for people faithful /
suppose I call-out, he hear me
Lord, please your face shine-on-me / my heart inspire happy.

Happen I lie-down / I feel peace, fall-asleep
Lord, only-you / give me home safe.

FIRST LETTER OF JOHN (2:1–5a)

My friend, I write for-for? Help-you sin avoid. But suppose you sin, Jesus face-to-face Father, ask-him forgive you. Jesus finish die for our sin and for #ALL people sin. Know God true can we—how? His commandments obey. Suppose person say, "I know God" but commandments he obey not, lie he; honest none. But suppose person obey God, his (God) love perfect inspire him (person).

GOSPEL ACCLAMATION

Alleluia

Lord Jesus, Bible please explain for us
Teach-us, our heart inspire.

HOLY GOSPEL ACCORDING TO LUKE (24:35–48)

Disciples two-of-them story recent happen there town name <u>Emmaus</u>—bread Jesus tear-apart, give-out; oh-I-see, they know who he. Wrong, Jesus himself appear, said, "Peace, you." They afraid! Think ghost. Jesus said, "You afraid, why? Silly. My hands, feet look-at, that's me (hon). Come, touch-me. Ghost have skin, bone, none." Hands, feet he show-them.

They still shock, happy. Jesus question-them, "Food have?" Fish give-him, see Jesus eat. Finish, Jesus tell-them, "Everything I teach you up-to-now, remember must you. Moses, prophet write about me, now whole-thing satisfied, finish." Bible scriptures Jesus explain, they understand clear, quote: "Messiah suffer, die, third day resurrect. Now #ALL country you (apostles) preach must, tell-them pray for-for? sin theirs God forgive. Start Jerusalem, spread. True witness, you."

Gospel his Lord.

Fourth Sunday of Easter

ACTS OF THE APOSTLES (4:8–12)

<u>Peter</u>, himself Holy Spirit inspire, announce: "You leaders, you want us explain how man past crippled now healed, walk can, how possible. You and Israel people must understand we cause-him heal how? Name [of] Jesus from <u>Nazareth</u>, that-one Jesus you crucify, he die, God raise-him live again. His name power heal, man crippled now fine. Jesus himself, quote, 'Stone, it builders reject, now become most important support.' Other person save us, have none why? Other name have power, none."

Word his Lord.

RESPONSORIAL PSALM (118:2, 8–9, 21–23, 26, 28, 29)

Stone, it builders reject, itself now most important support.

Thank Lord, himself good / his mercy continue forever
Trust Lord (l), trust man (r) / it, trust Lord, better
Trust Lord (l), trust king (r) / it, trust Lord, better.

Lord I thank-you, why? You answer-me / you save me
Stone, it builder reject / itself now most important support
Lord himself finish cause / we see, wonderful.

Bless him, come name Lord / we honor-you (God) here temple
I thank-you, why? You answer-me / you save me.
Thank Lord, himself good / his kindness continue forever.

FIRST LETTER OF JOHN (3:1–2)

You see God love us so-much, name-us his children. We his children true~work. World accept us not—why? World recognize, accept Jesus never up-to-now. But we true God his children now. Future—?

Wait, let's-see. We know-that future we become same-as God. See-him true honorific (hon), will we.

Word his Lord.

GOSPEL ACCLAMATION

Alleluia

Lord says, Myself good shepherd,
My sheep, I know them, same-same they know me.

HOLY GOSPEL ACCORDING TO JOHN (10:11–18)

Jesus said, "Myself good shepherd—why? Die for my sheep willing me. Suppose hire worker, he care-for sheep, himself have sheep none, he don't-care. Happen wolf show-up, he escape, sheep abandon. Wolf catch, swallow can; sheep scatter. Reason? He work for money. He cherish sheep nothing.

"Myself good shepherd. My sheep, I know them, same-same they know me. Compare same Father know me and I know Father. Die for my sheep willing me. Other sheep I have, not here; lead them must I, my voice they hear, follow-to-here, become combined one group, one leader. Father love me—why? I willing die, resurrect live again. None force-me. I volunteer. I have power die and power resurrect live again. That-one Father order me."

Gospel his Lord.

Fifth Sunday of Easter

ACTS OF THE APOSTLES (9:26–31)

Jerusalem <u>Saul</u> arrive, interact-with apostle group want, but they dread-him. He true disciple, they skeptical. Well, <u>Barnabas</u> introduce him, explain how he (Saul) travel, see Lord, talk-with-him; since, he brave preach about Jesus there city name <u>Damascus</u>, fear none. <u>Saul</u> stay with them there Jerusalem, open preach about Jesus. Those Jews speak Greek, he debate-them. They #do-do? Try kill-him. Other apostles hear their Greek plan, take-him (Saul), send-to city name <u>Tarsus</u>, safe.

Time~same, all-over-area, church have peace; increase; improve honor Lord. Holy Spirit help, influence-them.

Word his Lord.

RESPONSORIAL PSALM (22:26–27, 28, 30, 31–32)

Lord, I praise you face-to-face your people.

My promise I satisfy face-to-face people themselves honor Lord /
People humble eat, fill-up
Search-for Lord, praise him / your soul live forever.

People all-over earth remember Lord, look-at-him / Family there, there bow-down, honor-him.
People they finish die, bury, they honor-him / body dissolve, no-matter they bow-down.

My soul, he-give-me life / my children generations serve him.
Children born, / teach-them about Lord
They continue teach about God his judge~fair.

FIRST LETTER OF JOHN (3:18–24)

My friends, please show love true, not only talk about love. Suppose we love true, means honest we cherish, feel peace united God, no-matter guilty sin. Our sin, God knows. Our guilt, he removes. Suppose we guilty none, we know-that God himself with us. We pray these-things (on fingers), God give-me—why? Because his commandment we obey, action right. His commandment what? (1) Believe name his son, Jesus Christ, (2) love each-other same he command. Suppose you obey commandments couple, you, God, united. We can know two-of-us (God and me) united, how? Holy Spirit God give-me, put-in-heart.

Word his Lord.

GOSPEL ACCLAMATION

Alleluia

Lord says, "Connect-to me, two-of-us relationship must, why? Relationship, you work succeed will."

HOLY GOSPEL ACCORDING TO JOHN (15:1–8)

Jesus tell apostles, "Myself true grape plant; my Father himself farmer. Suppose one branch none grapes, he cut-off, throw-away; but suppose grapes have, he take-care, try increase grapes. You ready grow—why? My word I teach-you. Live connect me. Suppose branch break-off, it grow fruit can't. Same suppose two-of-us disconnect, you succeed can't. Myself plant, you branches (cl). Suppose two-of-us connect, you work++ succeed will, but suppose disconnect, you work++ worthless. Suppose person connect-me not, he compare branch dry, dead, throw-in-fire. Suppose you live connect-me, my words you memorize, happen you pray, God answer. You give-God glory—how? Become my disciple and work++ succeed."

Gospel his Lord.

Sixth Sunday of Easter

ACTS OF THE APOSTLES (10:25–26, 34–35, 44–48)

<u>Peter</u> enter house man name <u>Cornelius</u>, himself kneel-down, worship (to Peter). <u>Peter</u> tell-him, "Rise, myself man same-as-you." <u>Peter</u> proceed preach, "Now I understand true God have none favorite cherish people. Any person honor God, action right, God accept him." Wrong, Holy Spirit flutter-down, touch++ those people #ALL. Those believers themselves finish circumcise, they surprised Holy Spirit influence those non-Jews same-as-them. They (Gentiles) start new language speak, glory give-to God. Jews, <u>Peter</u> question-to-them: "Those people (Gentiles) finish receive Holy Spirit same-as-you. Baptize them, why~not?" So, order (Jews) them (Gentiles) baptize name Jesus Christ. Finish, they ask <u>Peter</u> stay day few.

Word his Lord.

RESPONSORIAL PSALM (98:1, 2–3, 3–4, 5–6)

All-over earth, people see God expert save.

New song sign-ASL-to Lord / he finish wonderful action
His right hand win succeed / himself mighty.

#ALL people Lord himself save / #ALL countries his judge~fair he show-around
He up-to-now kind, faithful / people Israel he cherish.

People all-over earth / finish see God save us
#ALL country sing happy for Lord / sign-ASL, praise.

FIRST LETTER OF JOHN (4:7–10)

Cherish friends, love each-other, why? Love itself come from God. Any person love, he connect God, he know God. Suppose person love none, he don't-know God, because God is! love. God show-you his love, how? His only Son he send-to world for give-you life. Love means what? We love God—shhh. God love us, his son send die for our sin.

Word his Lord.

GOSPEL ACCLAMATION

Alleluia

Lord says, Any person love me, my commandment he obey
My Father love him, two-of-us come-to-him.

HOLY GOSPEL ACCORDING TO JOHN (15:9–17)

Jesus tell apostles, "Father love me, same I love you. Continue my love show. My love you show, how? My commandments obey, same Father his commandments I obey, and his love I show. I tell-you these-things (on fingers), why? My happy share-with-you, same-as-me. My commandment? Love each-other, same I love you. Love~most means willing die in-exchange friends. You-all true my friends, understand, my commandment you obey. I name-you slave, no, because slave don't-know what boss~most #do-do. I name-you friend, because everything Father inform-me, I inform-you. You choose-me? No. I choose you—for-for? Go, action good succeed. Your good work continue must; finish, you ask Father these-things (on fingers), understand, use my name, he give-you. I command you only-one: Love each-other."

Gospel his Lord.

Ascension of the Lord

ACTS OF THE APOSTLES (1:1–11)

My first letter explain everything Jesus action, teach up-to-now, until day Jesus ascend heaven. First, apostles Jesus choose++, understand, Holy Spirit help-him; finish, teach-them++. Jesus suffer, die, resurrect finish, prove himself still alive. How? During 40 days, Jesus show-up from-time-to-time, story about kingdom his God. One time, Jesus tell-them "Stay here Jerusalem, wait Father his promise true happen. Up-to-now, John, he baptize water, but near-future few days Holy Spirit inspire-you."

Apostles question-him, "Lord, control you give-to Israel now?" Jesus answer, "Exact time, don't-know. Father himself know. Happen Holy Spirit influence-you, you strong will; finish, preach about me here Jerusalem, [there Judea and Samaria] all-over earth must you." Finish, Jesus ascend~dissolve.

They continue look-up; wrong, men two, clothes white, tap-on-shoulder, "You stand, look-up, for-for? Jesus, himself recent ascend, same #BACK will."

Word his Lord.

RESPONSORIAL PSALM (47:2–3, 6–7, 8–9)

God take-control, we shout happy, blow-horn loud for God.

You people, celebrate / shout happy for God
Lord most high, wonderful / himself king control earth.

God take-control, people shout happy / blow-horn loud for God
Praise sing for God, sign-ASL / praise sing for our king, sign-ASL.

God himself king control earth / praise sing, sign-ASL
God control #ALL countries / God holy throne sit.

LETTER OF PAUL TO THE EPHESIANS (4:1–13)

Myself now stuck prison, reason? I preach Lord. I encourage you continue live right, humble, gentle, patient; love, accept each-other; your spirit united-around, peace: only-one body, only-one spirit, only-one hope: have one Lord, one faith, one baptize, one God, himself Father [of] #ALL, himself control #ALL.

Each person, God give grace from Christ. Bible write, quote, "He finish ascend, prisoner he take-up, men he give-them wonderful."

Quote, "he finish ascend" mean what? Well, first he descend (cl:1) here earth. Descend finish, he ascend, touch heaven, now everything he control.

Some people he appoint become apostle, some prophet, preacher, teacher, for-for? Minister care-for people, Christ his body~group grow, become faith united-around, know Jesus Son (of) God, become mature Christians.

Word his Lord.

or

LETTER OF PAUL TO THE EPHESIANS (1:17–23)

God himself true Father glory. Please he give-you spirit wise, oh-I-see, help-you know him clear. Please he help-you understand (1) wonderful hope he offer-you, (2) glory he give-you share, (3) his power whew! in us believers. Same power God use raise-up Christ, put-him-on-right there heaven, every controller and angel exceed, every name now and future exceed. Everything God put under Christ control; himself compare head, church compare body. Through us, he influence whole world.

Word his Lord.

GOSPEL ACCLAMATION

Alleluia

Lord says, quote, "Go, #ALL countries teach;
Myself accompany-you always, until world collapse, dissolve."

HOLY GOSPEL ACCORDING TO MARK (16:15–20)

Jesus tell disciples eleven, quote, "All-over world go, announce good #NEWS. Suppose person believe, baptize, save he; suppose believe refuse, hell. How know who have faith? They use my name, devil eliminate. They speak language new, different. Snake, pick-up can. Poison drink, die none. People sick, they touch, heal them."

Jesus lecture finish, ascend heaven, with God. Eleven disciples spread-out, preach++. Lord continue support, their inform prove, how? Wonderful happen++.

Gospel his Lord.

Seventh Sunday of Easter

ACTS OF THE APOSTLES (1:15–17, 20a, 20c–26)

<u>Peter</u> stand face-to-face Christians, altogether approximately 120, hordes, said, "Brother++, long-ago Holy Spirit speak through <u>David</u>, predict about <u>Judas</u>, he lead soldiers arrest Jesus. True happen. He, <u>Judas</u>, past connect us, ministry share. Book Psalms says, quote, "Other person replace-him must." Right, we must choose someone himself past accompany, socialize during Lord Jesus still here alive, why? he can prove Jesus true resurrect." They nominate two, (1) <u>Joseph</u> [other name <u>Barsabbas</u>, other name <u>Justus</u>] and (2) <u>Matthias</u>. They pray, quote, "Lord, their hearts, you know. Please you show-me which one you choose for replace <u>Judas</u>, that-one backslide, go-astray." Those-two men close-eyes-draw-straw, who win? <u>Matthias</u>. He join-in, become apostle.

Word his Lord.

RESPONSORIAL PSALM (103:1–2, 11–12, 19–20)

Lord himself kind, mercy, angry not-yet, love excessive.

My soul honor Lord / his holy name I praise
My soul honor Lord / his benefit I remember (on fingers).

Earth, heaven high far / same-as people love him, his love excessive
East, west opposite far / same-as our sin God take-from-left, throw-to-right.

Lord his throne there heaven / his kingdom control whole-thing
You angels, honor Lord / yourselves mighty, no-matter,
his command you obey.

FIRST LETTER OF JOHN (4:11–16)

Cherish friend, God loves us so-much, same must we love each-other. Who finish see God? None! But suppose other people we love, God live in us; his love become perfect in us. We know God, two-of-us united, how? His spirit he give-us. Father send son for save world, we finish see, we prove can.

Suppose person accept Jesus true son his God, God live relationship-with-him (person and God). We now know and believe God love us. God himself true love. Any person show love, he, God, relationship.

Word his Lord.

GOSPEL ACCLAMATION

Alleluia

Lord says, I leave you alone, no-wave,
#BACK-to-you will I, happy will you.

HOLY GOSPEL ACCORDING TO JOHN (17:11b–19)

Jesus (look up) pray, "Father most holy, please you protect them, they can become united-around same we-two united. During I with-them, I protect them, use your name, that-one you gave me. I careful, lose none—shhh, lose one for Bible satisfy. Now I face-to-face-you, pray; they here, look-at-me I want, why? My happy share-with-them full. Your word I give-them, now world hate-them. They connect world not, same I connect world not. I not ask-you take-them-up out-of world, no. I ask-you devil protect-them. They same-as-me cherish world not. Cause-them holy through honest—your word true honest. Finish you send me here world, now I send them scatter world. I sacrifice myself now, why? Help-them become holy."

Gospel his Lord.

Pentecost Sunday

ACTS OF THE APOSTLES (2:1–11)

Day Pentecost, apostles assemble together. Wrong happen, noise compare strong-wind through house blow. Afraid! Surprise, show-up fire, fire-separate, each apostle fire-over-head (cl: 1,4). #ALL inspire Holy Spirit, begin lecture language different++ what Holy Spirit urge. Time~same there Jerusalem have Jew from every country assembled. Noise they hear, flock-to see what. Puzzled, why? Each++ hear apostles speak language his++ . Shock, said, "Those men from Galilee, right? How happen language his++, my, we hear, how? We come here from country many different++ [Judea, Pontus, Asia, Egypt, Libya, and many more other place]. Also visitor from Rome. #ALL themselves Jew #OR finish connect Jew religion. But each++ hear them speak his++ language about wonderful work God succeed."

Word his Lord.

RESPONSORIAL PSALM (104:1, 24, 29–30, 31, 34)

Lord, your spirit send-down, all-over earth become new.

My soul honor Lord / God, yourself wonderful true
Many things God make+++ / earth hordes he make.

Suppose breathe, you stop-it / they die, dissolve
Happen your spirit touch, they live / all-over earth become new.

Lord his glory continue forever / Lord make++, satisfy
My song, Lord enjoy / I happy connect-to-him.

LETTER OF PAUL TO THE GALATIANS (5:16–25)

Brother~sister, live follow spirit must; body lust, resist. Body, spirit, opposite, struggle. You goal want action right, frustrate, fail.

But #IF spirit you follow, law not~need. Body, its actions easy notice—what? (left) Sin, lust, idol worship, magic, hate, argue, jealous, anger, selfish, clash, disagree, thirst~want, drinking-alcohol, #SEX, various. Warning! These-things (on fingers) you follow? Touch heaven never.

Compare, Holy Spirit give what? (right) Love, happy, peace, patience, kindness, willing give, faithful, heart~soft, self~control. These-things (on fingers), law prohibit not.

Suppose Christ you connect, your body finish crucify, die; sin list (on fingers) dissolve. Now live follow Holy Spirit.

Word his Lord.

or

FIRST LETTER OF PAUL TO THE CORINTHIANS (12:3b–7, 12–13)

You say, quote, "Jesus true Lord," how possible? Holy Spirit inspire-you. Have skill many various, but Spirit one; have ministry many various, but Lord one; have work many various, but God one, himself succeed everything. Each person have Holy Spirit inside for benefit #ALL same-around. Body itself one; hands, arms, feet, various have; no-matter, still body one. Christ compare same. #ALL people, no matter Jew, Greek, slave, free, no-matter, #ALL baptize become united quote "body" group one—how? Holy Spirit influence.

Word his Lord.

GOSPEL ACCLAMATION

Alleluia

Come, Holy Spirit, our heart touch,
Your love inspire.

HOLY GOSPEL ACCORDING TO JOHN (15:26–27, 16:12–15)

Jesus tell disciples: "Happen heaven I touch succeed, Holy Spirit, [name <u>Advocate</u>] I send-you will. Spirit himself full honest, inform-you honest about me will he. Same-same you inform-out about me, why? Two-of-us together up-to-now.

"More information have I, but you-all ready understand not-yet. Happen Holy Spirit touch-you, himself Spirit full honest, he teach-you will. Spirit himself invent++? No. I tell-him, he teach-you, plus he inform-you future happen++. Glory he give-me why? everything I tell-him he teach-you. Understand, everything Father tell-me, I tell-to Holy Spirit, he tell-to you."

Gospel his Lord.

or

HOLY GOSPEL ACCORDING TO JOHN (20:19–23)

Week, first day, night, apostles meet room, close-door, lock, why? Afraid Jew. Wrong, Jesus show-up, said, "Peace you." Show-them hands, side. Disciples look-at-Jesus, excited. (Jesus) "Peace, calm-down. Father long-ago send me, same now I send-you." Jesus breathe, exhale-on-them, said, "Holy Spirit I give-you. Suppose man sin, you forgive, I forgive succeed. Suppose you forgive refuse, sin stay."

Gospel his Lord.

Holy Trinity

BOOK OF DEUTERONOMY (4:32–34, 39–40)

People hordes, Moses tell-them, "Now mull-over time-period long-ago, about all-over earth. ? Wonderful things happen up-to-now? God voice speak from fire, long-ago people hear same you? Other god cherish people~group, other country save-them, show wonderful works—war mighty, action awful? These-things (on fingers), there Egypt, Lord your God action, yourselves finish see. Now must you know-that Lord himself God there heaven, here earth, other god have none. His law I teach you today, obey must you—why? You, your children generations-forward succeed will, long live there land God give-you."

Word his Lord.

RESPONSORIAL PSALM (33:4–5, 6, 9, 18-19, 20, 22)

Bless those people Lord pick++ for connect-to-him.

Lord his word right / his work we trust can
Judge~fair, good actions, he love / his kindness spread-over earth.

Lord speak, cause heaven, earth, set-up / he breathe, cause everything out-there
He speak, make! / He command, true happen!

Lord look-down, see people honor-him / he kind-to-them they hope,
Die, he save-them / hungry, he feed-them.

Our soul wait-for Lord / himself help-us, protect-us.
Lord, mercy-us / we trust-you.

LETTER OF PAUL TO THE ROMANS (8:14–17)

Suppose Holy Spirit you follow, means yourself child his God. God give-you slave spirit, cause-you fear? No, he give-you spirit become his children, cause-you cry-out "<u>Abba</u>," means "Father." Spirit himself prove we true children his God. Means what? God willing give-us everything, same Christ—understand, suffer with Christ must, finish, glory with Christ.

Word his Lord.

GOSPEL ACCLAMATION

Alleluia

Glory give-to Father, Son, Holy Spirit
God himself since, forever.

HOLY GOSPEL ACCORDING TO MATTHEW (28:16–20)

<u>Galilee</u>, disciples eleven group-go, mountain that-one Jesus tell-them meet-him. Jesus they see, kneel, honor-him. Jesus tell-them, "Full authority there heaven, here earth, God finish give-me. Now, your-turn go, #ALL people teach-them become my follower. Baptize them name Father, Son, Holy Spirit. Everything I order, you teach++. Know-that I continue accompany-you always, until world completed, dissolve."

Gospel his Lord.

Body and Blood of Christ

BOOK OF EXODUS (24:3–8)

Everything God order, Moses inform people. People #ALL answer, "Everything Lord order, we obey will." Lord tell Moses, he jot-down. Tomorrow morning, altar with pillar (cl:c, c) twelve he build, why? Israel have <u>tribe</u> twelve. Young men few, Moses tell-them bull kill, fire~sacrifice [to] Lord for peace. Finish, blood left-there, Moses separate half-half. Point-left blood, bowl, scoop-blood-in, set-aside. Point-right blood, scoop-up, splash-on altar, splash-on. Now Moses open-book, law his God teach. People say, "Everything Lord order, we obey will." Blood~point-left, Moses scoop-up, sprinkle-on people, say, "This blood mean God, you-all promise~united; understand, his law you obey."

Word his Lord.

RESPONSORIAL PSALM (116:12–13, 15–16, 17–18)

Wine cup itself save, I drink; Lord his name I summon

Many good things Lord give-me / I thank-him how?
Cup wine, I drink / his name, I summon.

Faithful people die / Lord, see cherish
Myself your servant / you give-me free.

Sacrifice, thanks, I offer-to you / Lord his name, I summon
Promise I give-to Lord / #ALL people see.

LETTER TO THE HEBREWS (9:11–15)

Christ himself priest~most, good things he-give-us. Holy place there heaven he finish enter, here earth not. Blood its animal, Jesus not~need. His blood save us. Blood from goat, bull, kill, fire~sacrifice, it cause body become holy, but Christ finish sacrifice himelf; he perfect, sin none. Means what? His blood cause mind, heart become clean, possible we worship God true. New promise~united Jesus give. Old promise~united, we sin, disconnect. Jesus die for-for? Save us, our sin forgive. Now we live with him there heaven forever can.

Word his Lord.

GOSPEL ACCLAMATION

Alleluia

Lord say, Myself live bread, heaven come-down (cl:1)
This (hon) bread you eat, live forever.

HOLY GOSPEL ACCORDING TO MARK (14:12–16, 22–26)

Almost near time celebrate lamb sacrifice for Passover, disciples ask-to Jesus, "We prepare Passover food where?" Jesus choose disciples two, tell-them, "Go city, notice man have jar (cl) full water. Follow-him—house he enter, two-of-you enter, say, 'Room for eat Passover with disciples his, Teacher curious, where?' He man will show-you room upstairs, large, table, chairs-around, nice. That room, two-of-you prepare." Disciples go (cl:v), arrive city, happen++ same Jesus predict. Food, two-of-them prepare. During eat, bread Jesus hold-up, bless, tear, give-them, said, "Here. This my body." Finish, wine Jesus lift-cup, thank-God, give-them, #ALL drink~pass. Jesus said, "This my blood, means promise~united. Blood I lose for-for? Many people save. Inform-you, wine I drink again never, until future day I drink wine new there heaven." They #ALL sing praise God; finish, mountain Olives group-go.

Gospel his Lord.

Second Sunday in Ordinary Time

FIRST BOOK OF SAMUEL (3:3–10, 19)

<u>Samuel</u> sleep there temple his Lord, <u>ark</u> [of] God (cl) there. Lord call-out; <u>Samuel</u> answer, "Here I (hon)." He run-to <u>Eli</u>, said, "What? You summon-me for-for?" <u>Eli</u> said, "I summon-you, nothing. Go sleep." (Samuel shrug), walk away (cl:1), get-in-bed, sleep. Again, Lord call-out, (Samuel) wake-up, (cl:1) walk-to-Eli, "What?" (Eli) "I summon-you not. Go sleep." Understand, <u>Samuel</u> know Lord not-yet. Third time Lord call-out, (Samuel) wake-up, sigh, (cl:1) go-to-Eli. "You summon me, why?" Succeed (pah!) <u>Eli</u> understand Lord himself call-out. Tell <u>Samuel</u>, "Go, sleep. Suppose again hear call-out, you say "Speak, Lord, your servant pay-attention." (Samuel) Walk away (cl:1), get-in-bed, sleep. Lord arrive, his (Samuel's) name call-out. He wake-up, say, "Speak, Lord, your servant pay-attention." <u>Samuel</u> grow-up, Lord accompany, help-him speak influence.

Word his Lord.

RESPONSORIAL PSALM (40:2, 4, 7–8, 8–9, 10)

Here I (hon), Lord, your want, I obey.

I since wait++ Lord / he look-at-me, my call-out [he] pay-attention
New song he give-me / sign-ASL for God.

Animal kill, sacrifice, you don't-want / you want what? My obey
Animal fire-up for you forgive me, you don't-want / now I come, obey

Bible write / it inform-me
Your want obey give-me happy / your law my heart
jot-down-on-heart

You judge fair, I announce / #ALL people I inform
I shh, restrain-myself not / Lord, you finish know.

FIRST LETTER OF PAUL TO THE CORINTHIANS (6:13–15, 17–20)

Our body sin, better not. Our body, Lord himself, united. God finish raise-up Jesus, same raise-up us will he. ? Know~that your body united Christ? Person himself united Lord, his spirit united same. Dirty action, push-aside. Other sin touch body not, but sex sin hurt body. You know-that your body compare temple—why? Holy Spirit inside—that-one spirit God give. You #OWN yourself not. God finish buy you, whew! High cost. Well, use your body for glory give-him.

Word his Lord.

GOSPEL ACCLAMATION

Alleluia

We finish find Messiah, Jesus Christ
Himself give-us honest, grace.

HOLY GOSPEL ACCORDING TO JOHN (1:35–42)

John Baptist there Bethany with friend two. Notice Jesus (cl:1) walk-by, said, "Hey, there Lamb [of] God!" Two-of-them follow (cl:V,1), Jesus look-back, two-of-them follow for-for? Question-to-them, "Search-for what?" (disciples) "Rabbi [means Teacher], you stay where?" (Jesus) "Come, see." Two-of-them accept, follow, see where Jesus live, stay all-afternoon, time 4:00, all-afternoon. Two-of-them, one name Andrew. His (Andrew) brother name Simon. He (Andrew) run, find Simon, inform-him, "Two-of-us finish find Messiah!" Two-of-them go (cl:V), meet Jesus. He (Jesus) look-him-up-and-down, said, "Yourself name Simon, [son of John]. Now your name change Cephas, means Peter."

Gospel his Lord.

Third Sunday in Ordinary Time

BOOK OF JONAH (3:1–5, 10)

<u>Jonah</u>, Lord inform-him, "City name <u>Nineveh</u>, go, announce same I tell-you." <u>Jonah</u> ready, go-out. Understand, <u>Nineveh</u> itself large city, walk through require three-days. <u>Jonah</u> start walk, announce, quote, "Forty days left, God destroy city will." First day finish, people believe God, decide fast, plus #ALL people, no-matter important, trivial, no-matter, #ALL must put-on <u>sackcloth</u>. God see their #do-do, their sin sorry, push-aside, he heart~soft, destroy not.

Word his Lord.

RESPONSORIAL PSALM (25:4–5, 6–8, 8–9)

Lord, your way teach-me.

Lord, your way show-me / your way teach-me
Lead-me [to] your honest / yourself my savior true.

Lord, remember your mercy / yourself kind up-to-now
Please you remember me / because yourself good.

Lord true~work good, right / sinners, right way he show-them
People humble, he lead, judge-fair / his way, he teach-them.

FIRST LETTER OF PAUL TO THE CORINTHIANS (7:29–31)

I inform-you, time used-up. From-now-on, wife have? Live idea-same single. Cry? Live idea-same happy. Celebrate? Live idea-same sad. You buy++? Live idea-same have nothing. World you take-advantage? Live hands-off—why? World itself dissolve will.

Word his Lord.

GOSPEL ACCLAMATION

Alleluia

God his kingdom near-future establish.
Your life change, gospel believe.

HOLY GOSPEL ACCORDING TO MARK (1:14–20)

<u>John</u> arrest, jail; finish, Jesus go <u>Galilee</u>, announce, "Now right time. God his kingdom near. Sin sorry, push-aside; good #NEWS believe."

Jesus walk (cl:1) near ocean, notice <u>Simon</u> and brother <u>Andrew</u>, two-of-them <u>net</u> (cl:4,4) throw-out, pull-in, fish recruit. Jesus said, "Come, follow me. People recruit, I teach you." Two-of-them quick abandon, follow. Three-of-them (cl:3) walk; Jesus notice <u>James</u> and brother <u>John</u> with father. Two-of-them boat, work. Jesus call, two-of-them abandon father, boat, depart, follow Jesus.

Gospel his Lord.

Fourth Sunday in Ordinary Time

BOOK OF DEUTERONOMY (18:15–20)

<u>Moses</u> inform people, "Other person become prophet same me, Lord God pick will. Pay-attention-him—why? Past, there <u>Horeb</u>, meeting day, you pray, said, 'Again hear voice his Lord, we don't-want; see fire, don't-want, afraid die.' Well, Lord tell-me, 'Those people pray good, right. Pick prophet same you will I; inform-him; he inform people will. Suppose he inform same I tell-him, and person himself pay-attention refuse, punish him (person) will I. But, suppose prophet inform something different, I tell-him not-yet, die will he (prophet).'"

Word his Lord.

RESPONSORIAL PSALM (95:1–2, 6–7, 8–9)

Suppose today God speak you feel, pay-attention, ignore not.

Come, happy sing for Lord / himself our support, our Savior
Come face-to-face him, thank-you / happy sign-ASL.

Come, bow-down, worship / kneel face-to-face Lord,
he finish make us
He true our God / we people he care-for, protect.

I hope today God speak, you feel / ignore not, same long-ago
There desert your ancestors doubt / God wonderful work they see, no-matter, skeptical.

FIRST LETTER OF PAUL TO THE CORINTHIANS (7:32–35)

I wish worry dissolve. Man married not-yet, he work++ serve Lord. Man married finish, he busy, work++ care-for wife. He on-the-fence, stuck. Woman married not-yet, concentrate Lord, herself body and spirit holy. Woman finish married, she concentrate world, care-for husband. I explain++ for your benefit. Marry prohibit, don't-want me; but encourage good actions, help-you concentrate Lord, that-one I want.

Word his Lord.

GOSPEL ACCLAMATION

Alleluia

People past dark, now see wonderful light;
Past live land obscure, now light-shine-down.

HOLY GOSPEL ACCORDING TO MARK (1:21–28)

City name Capernaum, temple Jesus enter, teach. People fascinate—why? Jesus teach authority, not same Jew teacher.

Happen man show-up, inside-body have spirit bad. Spirit cry-out, "What you want, Jesus? Destroy us you want? I know-that you true God his Son!" Jesus bawl-out: "Quiet! Out-thumb!" Man fall-down, seizure; spirit cry-out, go-out. People see, amazed, puzzled. "What~mean? He teach new, authority. Spirit he order out-thumb, spirit obey." That minute from-now-on, Jesus his story spread-all-over.

Gospel his Lord.

Fifth Sunday in Ordinary Time

BOOK OF JOB (7:1–4, 6–7)

Job said, "Life here earth means every-day work++ same slave; he wish tree sit-under, cool, wait-for pay-him. Me same, month++ grief, all-night restless me. Night, I get-in-bed, eyes-wide-open, sleep can't, wait sunrise, time get-up. Day spend, quick; finish, left hope none. Remember, my life compare wind++ dissolve. I happy again, never me."

Word his Lord.

RESPONSORIAL PSALM (147:1–2, 3–4, 5–6)

Praise Lord! People heart-wring, he give-them heal.

Praise Lord, himself good, sing praise God, himself kind /
Appropriate praise him
Jerusalem, again Lord build / people scattered, Lord collect

People their heart-wring, he heal / their hurt, he wrap-up, care-for
Count altogether how-many stars, he expert / each star name, he know.

Our Lord true wonderful, mighty / he wise awesome
People humble he support / people bad he throw-out.

FIRST LETTER OF PAUL TO THE CORINTHIANS (9:16–19, 22–23)

I preach gospel—boast me? No-wave, God force-me, none choice me. Preach refuse? Ruin me. Suppose I preach willing, I have my pay-me. Suppose preach don't-want, no-matter, duty! My pay-me what? Happen I preach, I give gospel free, cost none. Gospel give-me authority, I take-advantage not.

I slave, no, but I willing become slave for #ALL—why? Recruit++. Suppose he weak, I myself become weak same-as-him, recruit. #ALL people, I match++, recruit++. True, I action everything for help gospel spread—why? God bless me, hope.

Word his Lord.

GOSPEL ACCLAMATION

Alleluia

Our weak, Christ remove
Our sick, he take-from-me.

HOLY GOSPEL ACCORDING TO MARK (1:29–39)

Temple, Jesus depart, go-to house <u>Simon</u> and <u>Andrew</u> with friends few. <u>Simon</u>, his mother-in-law sick, bedridden. He inform Jesus she sick. Jesus walk-to-her (cl:1), take-hand, she-get-up, healed. She quick start serve.

Sunset, darken, people sick they bring++, some have devil inside-body. Soon, people hordes outside, all-eyes-looking-in (cl:4,4). People sick many, Jesus influence heal; also devil eliminate (r-l-r) many. Devil speak, prohibit, Jesus no-no (wag finger)—why? Devil know Jesus. Tomorrow morning early Jesus get-up, go (cl:1) quiet place alone, pray. <u>Simon</u> with friends few search, find [him], said, "#ALL people search-for you." Jesus said, "Come-here, we group-go next town, announce good #NEWS there can I. That-one reason I here."

All-over <u>Galilee</u>, Jesus touch++, good #NEWS preach, devil eliminate++.

Gospel his Lord.

Sixth Sunday in Ordinary Time

BOOK OF LEVITICUS (13:1–2, 44–46)

<u>Moses</u>, brother <u>Aaron</u>, God inform-them, quote, "Suppose person skin have spot++ (cl:f), sick name <u>leprosy</u>, #do-do? Aaron #OR other priest, put-him (r to l) face-to-face. Suppose he (man) true~ work sick <u>leprosy</u>, priest name-him quote 'not~clean.' He #do-do? Clothes tear, hood-back, face wrap, shout, 'Not~clean, me!' Why? Spot++ have, mean not~clean. He live separate must, town there (l), he live there (r), separate."

Word his Lord.

RESPONSORIAL PSALM (32:1–2, 5, 11)

Happen time-period trouble, I trust you Lord,
You give-me happy, save.

Bless that person his wrong remove / his sin forgive
Happy he, why? Lord blame-him not / his spirit innocent.

My sin I finish confess [to] Lord / my guilt I cover-up not
I tell-him, "My sin I confess" / my guilt, he remove.

You people good, connect Lord, celebrate / your heart honest, celebrate.

FIRST LETTER OF PAUL TO THE CORINTHIANS (10:31—11:1)

Brother~sister, suppose you eat, drink, various, everything action for-for? Glory give-to God. Jew, Greek, church itself insult++, no-wave. Become same-as me, every person satisfy, I try, why? Benefit myself—shhh. Save them. Christ I copy-from, you copy-from-me, he-give-me, I-give-you.

Word his Lord.

GOSPEL ACCLAMATION

Alleluia

Wonderful prophet here show-up.
God socialize-with his people.

HOLY GOSPEL ACCORDING TO MARK (1:40–45)

Man himself sick name <u>leprosy</u>, he kneel face-to-face Jesus, said, quote, "Heal me can you, think-self." Jesus pity-him, willing, lay-hands, heal! Spots++ (cl:f) dissolve, heal. Jesus strict inform-him, "Story recent happen, you tell, no-no (wag-finger). Priest there, you go show-him yourself clean~healed, finish, sacrifice same Moses order. People see, proof!"

Man depart, wrong, story++ recent happen, talk++, spread. Now, Jesus dare-me town enter, impossible. Jesus #do-do? Stay (opposite side), alone. But people flock-to-him, popular.

Gospel his Lord.

Seventh Sunday in Ordinary Time

BOOK OF THE PROPHET ISAIAH (43:18–19, 21–22, 24b–25)

Lord says, quote, "Long-ago happen++, dwell-on not, push-aside, why? New things I succeed. Now see! There desert, I make way; there dry, I cause river. Those people, I make for myself, for-for? My praise announce. But Israel people summon-me never. They ignore-me. They sin++, wrong++, bore me. But I think-myself, your wrong I forgive, your sin I forget."

Word his Lord.

RESPONSORIAL PSALM (41:2–3, 4–5, 13–14)

Lord, I finish sin. My soul please heal.

Bless person, he honor people poor, humble / happen he trouble, Lord save him
Lord care-for, protect-him, bless-him here earth / his enemies, God defend-him.

Happen he sick, laid-up, God help-him / his sick, God remove, heal
Past, I said, "God, please mercy-me / I finish sin, no-matter, please heal me."

Myself honest, well, God support-me / allow me with-him forever
Bless Lord, himself God for Israel / forever [and] ever, amen.

SECOND LETTER OF PAUL TO THE CORINTHIANS (1:18–22)

Brother~sister, I faithful same-as God himself faithful, on-the-fence not. God his son Jesus Christ, that-one three-of-us preach, he "yes," "no," "on-the-fence" not. He full #YES. God promise many (list-on-fingers), succeed will through Jesus. Our faith touch God, give-him glory through Jesus. But who cause two-of-us connect? Who choose three-of-us for preach? God himself. He finish inspire us, his holy Spirit give-us.

Word his Lord.

GOSPEL ACCLAMATION

Alleluia

Lord send-me here for good #NEWS inform-to people poor, People prison, now out free.

HOLY GOSPEL ACCORDING TO MARK (2:1–12)

Jesus arrive home. People many enthusiastic flock-to-him, crowded, house full. Jesus preach. Wrong, men four carry (mime carrying stretcher), man lay-there, himself paralyzed. Stuck, traffic (cl:5,5), #do-do? Look-up, roof. Decide carry-up, open, let-down (mime). Jesus (look up), faith wow. (Look-down) tell-him, "Your sin forgive finish." Jew few there wonder, "Lie he. Sin forgive can't—only God himself expert forgive." Their thoughts, Jesus know, question-to-them: "You doubt, why? I say 'Your sin forgive' (l), 'Stand, walk' (r), easy which (point, point)? Equal. Authority for forgive sin have me—proof what? (to paralytic) I order, you stand up, go-away home." Quick, man stand up, bed pick-up, put-under-arm, go-away. People shock, glory give-to God, say, "We see before never!"

Gospel his Lord.

Eighth Sunday in Ordinary Time

BOOK OF THE PROPHET HOSEA (2:16b, 17b, 21–22)

Lord says, "Israel people~group, I lead-them there desert will I. Their heart I inspire. Finish, they will love me same long-ago, Egypt, happen I save them. Two-of-us united forever. Judge~fair, (2) honest, (3) love, (4) mercy establish will I. They continue faithful? Know Lord will."

Word his Lord.

RESPONSORIAL PSALM (103:1–2, 3–4, 8, 10, 12–13)

Lord, himself kind, mercy.

My soul celebrate Lord / his holy name I honor
My soul celebrate Lord / his benefits I remember, forget not.

Your sin, he forgives / your sick, he heals
Your life ruin, he protects / kind, mercy, he give-you.

Lord himself mercy, heart~soft / angry not-yet, kind excessive
Our sins he punish not / our wrong he get-even not.

East, west, far-apart / same our sin God take-from-left, throw-to-right
Children, father cherish / same those people honor God,
he cherish, same.

SECOND LETTER OF PAUL TO THE CORINTHIANS (3:1b–6)

Brother~sister, ?? Letter for introduce, prove, need me? You true my quote "letter," heart jot-down. #ALL people quote "read-you," know-that you united Christ same we preach, proof. Ink write-on-you? No, God his spirit influence-you. Rock square write-on? No, your heart accept. That-one, God give-me confident.

Understand, ourselves expert preach not, boast not. Our skill, God give-me; himself choose-me for preach law new—write, shhhh. Spirit only. Why? Law write, list-on-fingers gives die, but spirit gives live.

Word his Lord.

GOSPEL ACCLAMATION

Alleluia

Father give-us life, decide, think-himself
#ALL animals, we first-place, top.

HOLY GOSPEL ACCORDING TO MARK (2:18–22)

John Baptist, Pharisee, their disciples habit fasting. Jesus, people question-to-him, "Their disciples tend fasting, but your disciples fasting nothing—why?" Jesus tell-them, "Suppose wedding celebration, party—people eat refuse?? Husband still there, people eat must, fasting can't. Few days later, husband depart, people go-ahead fasting.

"Suppose old coat tear, new cloth put-on, sew? No, happen wash, new shrink, pull-apart worse. #OR, suppose old leather wine container (cl) have. New wine pour in? No, expand, pop. Wine lose, container ruin. New wine have? New container pour-in, fine."

Gospel his Lord.

Ninth Sunday in Ordinary Time

BOOK OF DEUTERONOMY (5:12–15)

Lord says, "Seventh day keep holy must you, same I finish command you. Six days you work++, but seventh day honor Lord your God must. Yourself work prohibit, plus, your son, daughter, man~woman slave, animals, other people live with you, they (on fingers) work prohibit, rest must. Remember long-ago there Egypt, yourself slave. Lord your God save you, lead you out free. Now, God order-you seventh day rest."

Word his Lord.

RESPONSORIAL PSALM (81:3–4, 5–6, 7–8, 10–11)

Happy sing sign-ASL-to God, our helper.

Sing, sign-ASL, tambourine tap-on-hip / harp (cl) sing
Moon new, trumpet-blow / happen moon (cl: L,L), we celebrate.

Israel, it have law / God himself order
Law, God give long-ago from-then-on / Egypt, Israel people bring~free.

I hear story, who speak, don't-know / quote "Your burden, I remove
Your work, I give-you free / you cry-out, I save you."

Quote "Future you have other gods none /
other god you worship never
I, myself Lord your God / there Egypt, I bring-you-out."

SECOND LETTER OF PAUL TO THE CORINTHIANS (4:6–11)

Brother~sister, God himself cause dark become light. Now our heart, he shine-on, his glory we can know, how? Jesus Christ. We know, yes, but our body weak. Our power show? No, God his power. We suffer, but give-up not. We puzzled, but depressed not. They persecute-me, but destroy-me not. My body same-as Jesus, die will; finish, my body same-as-him live again will. We live still, but always willing die for Jesus, why? Jesus his life inspire-me.

Word his Lord.

GOSPEL ACCLAMATION

Alleluia

Lord, your word itself honest
Please inspire-us honest.

HOLY GOSPEL ACCORDING TO MARK (2:23—3:6)

Seventh day, Jesus walk through field farm, disciples pick-and-put-in-bag. Pharisees see, say, "Saturday work, prohibit!" Jesus said, "You know story <u>David</u>, right? He, his friends hungry, #do-do? Church, enter, holy bread eat, that bread special for priest only. Seventh day God himself give-you, for-for? Rest. But myself Lord; obey, rest, not~need."

Synagogue, Jesus enter, see man there his hand shriveled (cl:claw). Pharisees watch (Jesus) let's-see he heal him now rest~day. Man, Jesus tell-him, "Come here (beckon)." (Jesus) Tell-them, "Action good (l), action bad (r), life save (l), life destroy (r), appropriate which? (point++)" They quiet (smugly). Their heart cold, Jesus know, feel angry, grief. Man, Jesus tell-him, "Your hand stretch-out." Man stretch-out-hand, healed.

Pharisees quick depart, meet <u>Herod</u> his followers, discuss, plan kill Jesus.

Gospel his Lord.

Tenth Sunday in Ordinary Time

BOOK OF GENESIS (3:9–15)

Tree, fruit, <u>Adam</u> eat; finish, Lord God call, "Where you?" (Adam) "You here <u>garden</u>, I hear, but afraid—why? I naked, hide." (God) "Oh-I-see. Who inform-you naked you? Maybe you eat fruit from tree that-one I prohibit?" (Adam) "Woman you put-here, she give-me fruit, so I eat." Lord God question-to woman, "You eat fruit—why?" (Woman) "Snake, he butter-up-hit. I eat." Snake, Lord God tell-him, "You awful action—punish what? From-now-on, #ALL other animals reject-you; you must crawl-like-snake (cl:1), soil eat. Self, woman, enemy. Your children, her children, enemy. Her son foot you bite (left bite right); he (right stomp on left)."

Word his Lord.

RESPONSORIAL PSALM (130:1–2, 3–4, 5–6, 7–8)

Lord himself have mercy, save us will he.

Myself suffer, I cry-out [to Lord] / my voice please pay-attention.
Lord, please pay-attention / my sign-ASL, my prayer.

Suppose Lord remember sin / who innocent, who?
But our sin you forgive / we honor-you, you want.

I trust Lord / his promise I believe.
Guard wait-for sunrise / same Israel wait-for Lord.

Lord himself mercy-us / save us he willing.
Israel he save, their sin forgive.

SECOND LETTER OF PAUL TO THE CORINTHIANS (4:13—5:1)

Brother~sister, Bible sentence, quote, "I believe, same-same I speak." We follow-it; we believe, same-same we speak. We know-that God finish raise-up Jesus live again, same he raise-up you, us, together with him will. Everything happen for benefit you—more, more people God bless, grace; you see, thank-him, glory give-him.

Means what? Discouraged, not~need. Body become old, ready die, but spirit become new, improve. Life difficult now, but future glory, wow! Here (l) we see, there (r) see can't; but it (l) dissolve will, it (r) continue forever. Our body itself compare tent, easy destroy; but God give-us new life forever there heaven.

Word his Lord.

GOSPEL ACCLAMATION

Alleluia

Past, devil control world, but now I defeat-him, Lord says. Happen cross lift-up, hang-on-cross, #ALL people I summon, come-here.

HOLY GOSPEL ACCORDING TO MARK (3:20–35)

Jesus with disciples there, many people flock-to, eat impossible. Jesus, his family hear story, think he crazy, decide to catch-him. Temple religious leaders, they think Jesus have devil inside, why? People there, there, there have devil spirit, he expert eliminate.

Leaders Jesus summon, question-to-them, "Devil eliminate other devil, how possible? Suppose kingdom people fight each-other, kingdom itself collapse will. Same family fight each-other, collapse will. So, suppose devil fight other devil, stand-strong can't, collapse will. Suppose strong man, his house you steal++ want, first man tie-him-up must; finish, steal can.

"Inform-you, people sin various, God insult, God forgive willing; but suppose person insult Holy Spirit [name <u>blaspheme</u>], forgive never." Understand, people gossip Jesus have dirty spirit, insult-God.

Now Jesus mother arrive with family, summon Jesus come. Friends tell-him, "Your mother, your family want you." Jesus answer, "My mother, family, who?" Look around. "You-all my true mother, family. Any person himself obey God, he my brother, sister, mother."

Gospel his Lord.

Eleventh Sunday in Ordinary Time

BOOK OF THE PROPHET EZEKIEL (17:22–24)

God said, "Tree grow (lh)—I will break-off-tip-and-hold (rh)—mountain (lh), plant-tip-on-top (rh), that mountain name Israel. Grow will it, grow, spread, fruit, large~tree. Bird various live there, make <u>nest</u> (cl:c,c). #ALL other trees know-that I, Lord, I cause important tree become worthless, humble tree become important, green tree wither, dead tree become alive bloom. I speak, same will I action."

Word his Lord.

RESPONSORIAL PSALM (92:2–3, 13–14, 15–16)

Lord, we thank-you, appropriate.

Now Lord we thank, appropriate / his name most high praise sign-ASL
Time sunrise, God kindness announce, / all-night his faithfulness announce.

Good man succeed compare tree strong / tall, strong, will he
Suppose Lord his house you cherish / succeed united God will you

Happen old, succeed still / strong, healthy, still
Announce Lord himself good / he support-me, himself wrong nothing.

SECOND LETTER OF PAUL TO THE CORINTHIANS (5:6–10)

We continue confident. We know-that life means Lord separate, but faith have, see-him not~need. We prefer body abandon, depart, go home with Lord. So, we try satisfy him, no-matter with or separate, no-matter. Future, our life Christ judge, pay each person fair, depend his life here earth, good, bad, which.

Word his Lord.

GOSPEL ACCLAMATION

Alleluia

#SEED, itself God his word; Christ sow-seed
Any person follow Christ, he live forever.

HOLY GOSPEL ACCORDING TO MARK (4:26–34)

Jesus tell people, "God his kingdom compare what? #SEED, man scatter, wait day, night, day, night. #SEED grow—how? Man don't-know. First little-bit grow (finger), later more grow, succeed <u>wheat</u>. Finish, time for harvest.

"#OR, God his kingdom compare what? What picture help-you understand? Compare <u>mustard</u> #SEED tiny, plant-it, grow, become big <u>bush</u>, many bird fly-to, make <u>nest</u> (cl:c,c)."

Jesus tell many stories, help-them understand; but apostles, Jesus private explain everything clear.

Gospel his Lord.

Twelfth Sunday in Ordinary Time

BOOK OF JOB (38:1, 8–11)

Man name J<u>o</u>b, Lord speak him: "Ocean, who close-door? Clouds for rain, I make; limit, close-door, lock I establish. Who tell water stay-here; spread-out, no!—who?"

Word his Lord.

RESPONSORIAL PSALM (107:23–24, 25–26, 28–29, 30–31)

Thank-you Lord, his love continue forever.

People ocean ride-in-boat / water deep
God his action they see / wonderful work there ocean.

God command, happen storm / water big-waves
Boat rise-high, drop-low / they heart-beat-fast, afraid.

They pray, cry-out / God see, save-them
Storm, he calm, quiet / ocean water calm-down.

They happy, celebrate / God bring-them safe arrive
Thank Lord, himself kind / he wonderful action for #ALL people.

SECOND LETTER OF PAUL TO THE CORINTHIANS (5:14–17)

Christ his love encourage us. We believe Christ finish die for #ALL, means #ALL finish die. Now live for myself? No, live for Jesus, himself die, resurrect finish.

From-now-on, judge people depend human way, finish. Past, we understand Jesus human way, but now different. Means what? Suppose any person connect Christ, that person himself become new. Old way push-aside, new way proceed.

Word his Lord.

HOLY GOSPEL ACCORDING TO MARK (4:35–41)

One day, time evening, Jesus tell apostles: "Water, we boat-cross-over." People~group, depart-from; boat, get-in, travel-by-boat. Wrong, hit storm. Boat, rock-side-to-side, water, big-waves. Jesus sit, sleep. Apostles tap-his-shoulder, "Wake-up! Drown near-future!" Jesus wake-up, tell wind, water~waves, "Finish! Quiet!" Wind, dissolve. Water, calm. Jesus tell-them, "You afraid, why? Faith none, you." They gulp, look-at-each-other, wonder, "Who he? Wind, ocean obey him."

Gospel his Lord.

Thirteenth Sunday in Ordinary Time

BOOK OF WISDOM (1:13–15; 2:23–24)

Death, die, God himself cause not. Suppose living things die, God celebrate not. #ALL living things God make, life give-them. Means what? Everything true~work good, none bad; devil things, earth have none. God judge fair forever. God finish make man for live forever, same God himself live forever. But devil, he jealous, cause people die. If you connect-to-him (devil), die will you.

Word his Lord.

RESPONSORIAL PSALM (30:2, 4–6, 11–13)

Lord, I praise you, why? You finish save me.

Lord, I praise you, why? You finish save me /
my enemy beat-me (shot-h), you prohibit
Die, you save me / people go-to hell, you grab-me-out.

You faithful people, sing praise Lord / thank-you his holy name
He angry short / but he mercy forever
Time night, cry / but sunrise, celebrate~happy.

Lord, please pay-attention-me, mercy-me / Lord, please help-me
Past, I heart-wring, now you give-me dance / I thank-you forever.

SECOND LETTER OF PAUL TO THE CORINTHIANS (8:7, 9, 13–15)

Yourselves expert faith, teach, know++, enthusiastic, love—please become expert give~share. You know-that Lord Jesus Christ, himself rich control everything, he willing become poor—why? Rich give-you. Means you money give-away, get-by must? No. Share equal. You have, he none, you share-with-him. Later, happen he have, you none, his-turn share-with-you. Long-ago write, quote, "Rich, poor, have equal."

Word his Lord.

GOSPEL ACCLAMATION

Alleluia

Die, Jesus Christ destroy
Life he give-us how? Gospel read.

HOLY GOSPEL ACCORDING TO MARK (5:21–43)

Sea [of] Galilee, Jesus cross-in-boat, arrive, people flock-to-him. Happen man name Jairus, himself temple leader, he meet Jesus, kneel, beg, "My daughter sick! Please you come touch-her, cause-her heal, live~continue." Two-of-them (cl:V) walk-away. People flock-to, follow (cl:5-wiggle).

There area woman, herself sick bleed menstrual-period up-to-now twelve years. Doctor different++ she go++, help none. Now, money used-up, woman sick worse. She hear story about Jesus, walk (cl:1)-through-crowd (cl:5-wiggle), think, "I touch-him, heal will." Put-hand-on-him (cl:1). Instantly, blood stop, heal. Jesus feel power out-of-him, look around (cl:f,f). "Who touch-me?" Disciples said, "People mill-around, you ask who touch-you??" Jesus, "phooey" point-around, Who?++ Woman, she scared, come (cl:1), kneel, inform honest. (Jesus) "Daughter, your faith cause-you heal. Go peace, sick push-aside, well from-now-on." Finish, people from house his temple leader, they arrive, inform-him, "Your daughter die finish. Bother Jesus, not~need." Jesus ignore-them. "Hey, fear worthless. Trust must you."

Peter, James, John, three-of-them go-with-Jesus (cl:3,1), others they follow, prohibit. (cl:3,1) approach-near house, noisy, people cry++, wail++. Jesus enter, said, "Cry++, cry-out++, for-for? Girl die not. Sleep she." People look-at-each-other, point-to-Jesus, "Pea-brain he." Jesus thumb-out. Mother~father, with Jesus, enter bedroom, girl lay. Jesus take-hand, say, "Girl, get-up." Girl, herself age 12, quick stand-up, walk-around. Family shock! Jesus scold, "Inform-them what happened, no! Oh, feed-her."

Gospel his Lord.

Fourteenth Sunday in Ordinary Time

BOOK OF THE PROPHET EZEKIEL (2:2–5)

Spirit inspire-me, force-me pay-attention. I feel someone inform-me, "Son of man, I send-you there Israel people, themselves rebel, oppose-me up-to-now. They true mean, stubborn people. You must tell-them, 'Lord God inform-you.' They pay-attention, resist, which? No-matter. They will know have prophet among-them, socialize."

Word his Lord.

RESPONSORIAL PSALM (123:1–2, 2, 3–4)

Lord we watch++, pray mercy-me.

I look-at you / throne there heaven
Compare slave / look-at boss.

Girl~servant / look-at controller
Same we look-at God / hope mercy-me.

Mercy-me, Lord, mercy-me / people mock-me, bore me
People arrogant make-fun-of / proud hate-me / fed-up me.

SECOND LETTER OF PAUL TO THE CORINTHIANS (12:7–10)

Wonderful things God show-me; but I become arrogant, he don't want. He give-me body problem from devil—why? Proud prevent. Three times I beg-him problem remove. He inform-me what? "My grace true support enough. Happen yourself weak, my power become perfect." Oh-I-see. Now I brag myself weak—why? Christ power inspire-me I want. No matter myself weak, insult-me, persecute-me, struggle, difficult, I accept because love Christ. Happen myself weak, that-one strong~most me.

Word his Lord.

GOSPEL ACCLAMATION

Alleluia

God his spirit inspire me,
he send-me for good #NEWS preach those people poor.

HOLY GOSPEL ACCORDING TO MARK (6:1–6)

Jesus with disciples his home area touch. Happen Sabbath, temple enter, begin teach++. Audience shock. "He learn++ where? Wise, expert he! Wonderful action, how? Himself carpenter, right? His mother Mary; his brother James, Joses, Judas, Simon, his sister live almost-nothing area, right?" They accept-him, can't (^). Jesus said, "Prophet, #ALL honor-him, but his friends, family honor-him not." Jesus wonderful work, impossible—understand, few people sick, Jesus lay-on-hands, heal, but other people faith none; Jesus disappointed, discouraged.

Gospel his Lord.

Fifteenth Sunday in Ordinary Time

BOOK OF THE PROPHET AMOS (7:12–15)

<u>Amos</u> there, priest name <u>Amaziah</u>, he tell-him, "You go-to <u>Judah</u>, work predict++, but predict here <u>Bethel</u> never again—why? Here king his home, his temple." <u>Amos</u> answer-him, "Up-to-now, I none predict; prophet group I socialize, nothing me. I work shepherd, also care-for tree <u>sycamore</u>. Sheep flock I watch, Lord take-me, he tell-me go, predict for his people Israel."

Word his Lord.

RESPONSORIAL PSALM (85:9–10, 11–12, 13–14)

Lord, your kindness allow us see, please save us.

God speak, I pay-attention / Lord announce peace for his people
People honor him, he save them / our country, his glory touch.

Kind (l), honest (r) connect / judge~fair (l), peace (r) spread-out
Here earth have honest / there heaven have judge~fair.

Lord himself bless us will / our land grow++ increase
God see, judge fair / prepare for himself come-down.

LETTER OF PAUL TO THE EPHESIANS (1:3–14)

Praise God, Father his Lord Jesus Christ. There heaven he finish bless us, how? Give-us Christ. Before world set-up, before, God choose us become holy, innocent, full love. Long-ago he plan adopt us become his children. That-one he want, why? Wonderful love he give-us through Jesus, #ALL people see, praise. Christ his blood save us, our sin forgive, God love give us. God give-us wise; plan he long-ago make with Christ we understand can, now true happen. What plan? #ALL things hand-over (cl:s) Christ control. God finish choose us.

He action think-self; his glory he want us praise, how? Christ trust. He choose you, when? time you first hear gospel, believe, accept Holy Spirit. He promise we future heaven. He finish save us, become God people; his glory we praise.

Word his Lord.

GOSPEL ACCLAMATION

Alleluia

God himself Jesus Father, please help-us understand,
Hope we have, why? God finish summon-us.

HOLY GOSPEL ACCORDING TO MARK (6:7–13)

Apostles twelve, Jesus summon, send++ couple++, halt!—first give-them authority devil spirit they control can. Jesus tell-them carry what? Stick (cl:f) for walk (mime); but other, (1) food none, (2) suitcase none, (3) money none. Shoes must, but other backup clothes none. House enter, stay until time leave go-to other town. Suppose people believe refuse, pay-attention refuse—depart. Shoes dust-off-hands, depart. Apostles patient go++ (cl:V, alt.), preach++, sick anoint oil, heal++ many.

Gospel his Lord.

Sixteenth Sunday in Ordinary Time

BOOK OF THE PROPHET JEREMIAH (23:1–6)

Lord says, "Awful those shepherds they. My sheep, they lead wrong way, scatter." Lord tell-them, "My people you finish scatter, care-for not. Punish-you will I. Land people scatter, myself gather++, bring-them here land, they increase++, expand succeed. Leader I pick++, care-for them, will I. They fear none, gone-from-sight none," Lord says. "Future I pick king good, right, himself David descendant. Control wise, fair all-over will he. That time-period, Judah safe, Israel live protect. Name-him what? Quote, 'Lord our judge~fair-er.'"

Word his Lord.

RESPONSORIAL PSALM (23:1–3, 3–4, 5, 6)

Lord himself my care-er, everything I need, he-give-me.

Lord himself my care-er, everything I need, he-give-me /
grass~area green he give-me rest
Quiet river near, he lead-me / my soul inspire

Right way he lead-me for his name honor / suppose dark valley
I walk (cl:1), no-matter, afraid not
God himself accompany, power protect-me / give-me brave.

Banquet he prepare for me / my enemy see
My head he oil anoint / he give-me plenty.

Only good, kind things touch-me during my life / Lord I connect, live together forever.

LETTER OF PAUL TO THE EPHESIANS (2:13–18)

You long-ago separate [from me], but now connect—how? Christ, his blood. He give peace, cause two-of-us become connect; past struggle, barrier push-aside, now harmony, connect. Christ die; law, commandment, rule he destroy. Two-of-us (2 people, cl:1,1), he cause meet, become one, united God. Two-of-us enemy, Christ defeat—how? Die cross. Christ come for announce good #NEWS, peace for people all-over. Now through one Holy Spirit #ALL face-to-face Father can.

Word his Lord.

GOSPEL ACCLAMATION

Alleluia

Lord says, My voice, my sheep hear,
I know them, they follow me.

HOLY GOSPEL ACCORDING TO MARK (6:30–34)

Apostles preach++ finish, flock-to Jesus, story everything happen++ up-to-now. Jesus said, "Come, group-go quiet place, rest." People many milling-around, they eat impossible. Jesus with apostles group-go, boat get-in-boat, boat-to quiet place. People see, gossip-around, decide flock-to-there, wait. Jesus arrive, see people hordes, feel~pity, why? Sheep have none care-er, they compare same. Jesus patient teach ++.

Gospel his Lord.

Seventeenth Sunday in Ordinary Time

SECOND BOOK OF KINGS (4:42–44)

Elisha, himself man connect God. Man from town far bring-to-him, give-him bread loaf 20 plus grain bag (cl) hand-to-him. Elisha tell-him, "Give-to people eat." Servant said, "This? One hundred men there." (Elisha) "Give-to people. Lord say, They eat, have left will." True enough, people eat++ finish, food left have, same Lord promise.

Word his Lord.

RESPONSORIAL PSALM (145:10–11, 15–16, 17–18)

Lord himself feed-us; we need, he give.

Lord, everything you make++, they #ALL thank-you / your faithful people honor you
Your kingdom glory, they story / your might, they announce.

#ALL people look-at you, hope / time right, food you give-them
Please give-us everything / our want satisfy.

Lord, he judge fair always / his work holy always
Suppose you pray, he near / understand, you pray honest.

LETTER OF PAUL TO THE EPHESIANS (4:1–6)

I up-to-now preach about Lord, now myself stuck prison. I beg-you live follow God his order—how? Humble, sweet, patient, accept each-other full love. Your spirit peace; try continue live connect-around. Have only-one body, only-one Spirit, only-one hope for #ALL. Have only-one Lord, only-one faith, only-one baptize. Have only-one God, himself Father for #ALL, control #ALL, work through #ALL, live in #ALL.

Word his Lord.

GOSPEL ACCLAMATION

Alleluia

Here have wonderful prophet
People here God touch.

HOLY GOSPEL ACCORDING TO JOHN (6:1–15)

Jesus boat-to, arrive Tiberias. People hordes follow, why? They see Jesus wonderful work heal people sick. Mountain, Jesus walk-up, sit with apostles. Time near Jew celebrate Passover. Jesus look-around, see people many!, question-to Philip, "Those people eat must—buy food where?" Understand, Jesus ready know what #do-do, but he want let's-see Philip answer. He (Philip) say, "Suppose have money exceed! Buy food for #ALL, impossible." One apostle, himself name Andrew, he say, "Here boy have bread five, fish few; but people hordes, it (food) worthless." Jesus said, "Tell people sit-down." Altogether approximately 5,000 men sit area grass. Bread, Jesus pick-up, pray thank-God, hand-out; fish same. People eat fill-up; finish, food left, collect, waste not. Collect how-much? Twelve baskets heap. Remember, only five bread, fish few. People see Jesus wonderful work, said, "Jesus true~work prophet, that-one we wait come-here world." Now, Jesus understand they intend grab-me, put me-up-high (cl:s), become king. Don't-want. Escape-to mountain, hide.

Gospel his Lord.

Eighteenth Sunday in Ordinary Time

BOOK OF EXODUS (16:2–4, 12–15)

Israel people complain, tell Moses, "We wish stay-there Egypt, eat, drink, satisfied. But you lead us here desert; hungry, die will we." God inform Moses, "I will cause bread from heaven snow-down. Every-day must people walk, gather; I watch-them, my order they obey, let's-see. They complain I finish hear. You tell-them, 'From-now-on, every-night meat eat, every-morning bread plenty eat. Why? You know-that Lord true God, will you.'"

From-then-on, every-evening camp there, birds hordes fly-over. Every-morning wet all-over, dissolve, dry, left white powder. Israel people see white dust, question, "What?" Moses explain, "Bread, Lord give."

Word his Lord.

RESPONSORIAL PSALM (78:3–4, 23–24, 25, 54)

Bread from heaven Lord give-them.

We finish hear, we know / our ancestors finish teach-us
Same our children we teach, / pass-forward, what?
Lord himself mighty, he action glory / he work wonderful.

Sky, he order / heaven, its door he open-door
Cause manna snow-down for their food / bread from heaven.

Angel bread, those people eat / food plenty
God lead-them here holy land / here mountain God give-them.

LETTER OF PAUL TO THE EPHESIANS (4:17, 20–24)

I inform-you, you continue live know-nothing, no! Christ teach-you live laid-back? No! I guess you finish learn honest about Jesus—

learn what? Your old life, itself worthless, sin, push-aside must; new life, holy think, begin from-now-on. Become person new must you, copy-God, live right, holy, honest.

Word his Lord.

GOSPEL ACCLAMATION

Alleluia

Bread alone give-you life, not enough
God his teach give-you life full.

HOLY GOSPEL ACCORDING TO JOHN (6:24–35)

People eat bread, finish, look-around—Jesus and disciples gone-from-sight. They decide get-in-boat, sail-to Capernaum, search-for Jesus. Find-him, question-him, "Rabbi, you arrive here when?" Jesus said, "You search-for me, for-for? Because proof you see? No! Because bread you eat fill-up. You search-for food itself run-out, no; search-for food itself continue forever. It food, Son [of] Man give-you, why? Father decide."

They question-him, "God his work we action how?" Jesus answer, "Have faith, believe God he send me (hon). That-one God work." (People) "Faith have—understand, you show proof. You #do-do, what? Our ancestors eat manna there desert. Bible story, 'Bread from heaven Moses give-them.'" Jesus inform-them, "Bread from heaven, Moses himself give not. My Father, he give true heaven bread. God bread from heaven give people life." They said, "That bread give-me always!" Jesus explain, "I myself bread of life. You connect-to-me, hungry again never. You believe me, thirsty never."

Gospel his Lord.

Nineteenth Sunday in Ordinary Time

FIRST BOOK OF KINGS (19:4–8)

<u>Elijah</u> travel one-day, desert arrive, notice <u>broom</u> tree, sit-under-it. Pray want die. "Lord, fed-up me. Please allow me die. Myself sinner, same my ancestors sinner." Finish, lay-down, fall-asleep. Later, angel go-to-him (cl:1), tap-shoulder, tell-him get-up, eat. (Elijah, groggy) Look around, there bread, there water <u>jug</u> (cl). Eat, drink finish, lay-down. Wrong, angel again tap-shoulder, said, "Get-up. Eat must. Long travel you." <u>Elijah</u> eat, drink; finish, feel strong, walk 40 day, night, arrive mountain his God, it name <u>Horeb</u>.

Word his Lord.

RESPONSORIAL PSALM (34:2–3, 4–5, 6–7, 8–9)

Taste, see, Lord himself good.

Lord I bless always, / praise sign-ASL forever
My soul have glory with Lord / people humble hear, celebrate

Two-of-us glory give-to Lord / together his name we praise
I search-for Lord, he answer-me / my fear, he remove.

Depend-on him, become happy, face-shine / you blush, ashamed, never
Have trouble, call-out-to him, he pay-attention / save you will he.

Angel from Lord come-down (cl:1), protect you, / understand, you know God
Taste, see, Lord himself good, / trust him, bless-you will he.

LETTER OF PAUL TO THE EPHESIANS (4:30—5:2)

Holy Spirit protect you; cause-him sad not. Jealous, hate, anger, criticize, sin list (on fingers), throw-out. Replace what? Kindness, mercy, forgive each-other, same God forgive you. You God his children. Follow his way. Christ love you, your-turn love each-other same. Christ sacrifice himself die for us; God accept, satisfied.

Word his Lord.

GOSPEL ACCLAMATION

Alleluia

Myself bread from heaven come-down (cl:1)
This (hon) bread eat, live forever.

HOLY GOSPEL ACCORDING TO JOHN (6:41–51)

Jew people complain, why? Jesus, he name himself, quote, "bread from heaven." Jews said, "That Jesus, his mother~father we know. He come from heaven, nothing!" Jesus tell-them, "Complain, finish! Suppose Father himself summon, persuade, you-all come-to-me—future last day, I raise-you-up. Long-ago prophet write, 'God himself teach-them.' Suppose Father you pay-attention, learn, you follow-me will. Yourselves see Father not-yet, but I see Father finish. I promise, suppose you believe, live forever you. I (hon) myself true bread of life. Your ancestors eat manna there desert, later die. This (hon) bread from heaven, you eat, die never. I myself true~work bread from heaven. Suppose this (hon) bread you eat, live forever. My bread, what? My body, for give-you life."

Gospel his Lord.

Twentieth Sunday in Ordinary Time

BOOK OF PROVERBS (9:1–6)

<u>Wisdom</u> (wise), itself build house, fine-wiggle. Meat cook, wine pour, table ready. Servant send-out all-over city, announce, "#ALL people humble, come-here. #ALL people understand not-yet, come, my food eat, my wine drink. Yourself know-nothing, no-matter. Come, your understand increase."

Word his Lord.

RESPONSORIAL PSALM (34:2–3, 4–5, 6–7)

Taste, see, Lord himself good.

Lord I bless always, / praise sign-ASL forever
My soul have glory with Lord / people humble hear, celebrate

Two-of-us glory give-to Lord / together his name we praise
I search-for Lord, he answer-me / my fear, he save me.

Depend-on him, become happy, face-shine / you blush, ashamed, never
Have trouble, call-out-to him, he hear / save you will he.

LETTER OF PAUL TO THE EPHESIANS (5:15–20)

Your #do-do, be-careful. Action silly, push-aside; become wise. Jump-at-the-chance must you—why? Now time-period bad. Continue know-nothing, no. Figure, try understand God his want. Wine get-drunk not, why? Cause-you sin. Yourself Holy Spirit filled-up; psalm holy sing together. Sign-ASL praise Lord; thank God Father always for everything, name Lord Jesus Christ.

Word his Lord.

GOSPEL ACCLAMATION

Alleluia

Any person my body eat, my blood drink,
two-of-us united, Lord says.

HOLY GOSPEL ACCORDING TO JOHN (6:51–58)

Jesus tell people, "I myself true bread from heaven. Suppose my (hon) bread you eat, live forever. I give-you bread, itself true my body, for give-you live." Jew people question, "His body give-us eat, how?" Jesus tell-them, "I inform-you, suppose my body you eat not, my blood drink not, life nothing you. Any person eat my body, drink my blood, he live forever. Future last day, I raise-him-up live again. My body true~work food; my blood true~work drink. Suppose person my body eat, my blood drink, two-of-us connect. Father send-me, life he give-me; same, person eat my body, life I give-him. This (hon) bread come from heaven. Your ancestors eat, later die; but suppose this (hon) bread eat, live forever."

Gospel his Lord.

Twenty-First Sunday in Ordinary Time

BOOK OF JOSHUA (24:1–2, 15–17, 18)

#ALL <u>tribes</u> there Israel, their priest, leader, judge, <u>Joshua</u> summon come-here meeting. He tell-them, "Serve Lord, don't want? Now decide, you serve who? Long-ago false <u>god</u>? Here <u>Amorite</u> their <u>god</u>? Fine. Me, my family, we decide serve Lord." People answer, "We ignore Lord, serve other <u>god</u>, never. Lord, himself our God; our family he bring out-of Egypt slavery. Wonderful work for us he action. During we travel through many country, he protect us. We same-as-you serve Lord, why? Himself true~work our God."

Word his Lord.

RESPONSORIAL PSALM (34:2–3, 16–17, 18–19, 20–21, 22–23)

Taste, see, Lord himself good.

Lord I honor always, / his praise I sign-ASL forever.
My soul have glory with Lord / people poor pay-attention, become happy.

People live right, Lord see-them / they cry-out, he pay-attention
People bad, Lord come-down, between-the-eyes / happen they die, friends forget.

Happen man poor suffer, Lord pay-attention / his trouble save-him
People suffer, Lord heart-touch / people heart-wring, he save.

Good man suffer many, true / but Lord save him always
God care-for him / his bones break none.

LETTER OF PAUL TO THE EPHESIANS (5:21–32)

[Care-for each-other for honor Christ. Wife obey husband idea~ same Lord, why? Husband compare head, wife his body; same

Christ head, church his body. Church obey Christ, same wife obey husband 100%.]

Husband, love your wife same Christ love church. Christ willing die for church—reason? Cause holy, become clean with baptize and his word. Finish, church itself full glory, holy, pure, sin none. Husband love his-own body, love wife same should he. Suppose wife you love, means you love self. Know-that no person hates his-own body. Every person eat, care-for body same Christ care-for church, why? We members his body connect. (quote) "Man his mother~father leave must, wife connect, two-of-them become one." That story show what? Christ, church, connect.

Word his Lord.

GOSPEL ACCLAMATION

Alleluia

Lord, yourself true~work spirit, life
your little-story give-me life forever.

HOLY GOSPEL ACCORDING TO JOHN (6:60–69)

Disciples few said, "Whew! Jesus story difficult accept. Doubt, me." They grumble, Jesus know. He question-them: "Skeptical you? Suppose you see me ascend heaven—what? Spirit, body, important which? It spirit give live. Body worthless. I up-to-now preach spirit and life, but some [of] you believe not-yet." [Jesus know who believe refuse. Jesus said,] "I finish tell-you, connect-me want? Father allow must." From-then-on, many followers un-popular, follow refuse. Apostles twelve Jesus question-to-them, "You escape, same?" Peter say, "Lord, we follow who? Your little-story give-us life forever. We believe strong yourself holy person from God."

Gospel his Lord.

Twenty-Second Sunday in Ordinary Time

BOOK OF DEUTERONOMY (4:1–2, 6–8)

Moses tell people, "Law I teach-you, pay-attention. Obey, live will you, plus land God give-you, enter~take-up. God his law obey 100%; none add, none subtract. You obey, prove yourselves wise, smart. Your law, other countries hear rumor, they say, 'Whew, Israel people true wise, smart.' Other country have its <u>god</u> close, where? Other country have law good, right same our law, where?"

Word his Lord.

RESPONSORIAL PSALM (15:2–3, 3–4, 4–5)

Person action right, he live with Lord.

That person innocent, / he action right
Honest dwell-on / lie never.

Other people, he hurt never / argue, dwell-on, clash not
Sinner he hate / good people he honor.

Money loan, interest charge none / money "under table" (toward self) accept for lie, never
Person action right these-things (on fingers) / live peace will he.

LETTER OF JAMES (1:17–18, 21b–22, 27)

Every good thing, every true benefit comes from Father there heaven. He change never, defeat-him never. Life he give-us, how? his word inspire, cause-us become his most important cherish. Now must you humble accept his word, itself have power save you. His command, obey. Listen only, action nothing, that worthless. Women, children they have father none, you care-for-them; sin not; finish, worship pure face-to-face Father can you.

Word his Lord.

GOSPEL ACCLAMATION

Alleluia

Father speak honest, give-us life
He make us most important, cherish.

HOLY GOSPEL ACCORDING TO MARK (7:1–8, 14–15, 21–23)

There Jerusalem, Pharisees and people themselves big-brains law came-to-here, Jesus meet (cl:5, 1). They finish notice Jesus his desciples~few eat, but wash-hands not-yet. Understand, Jews #ALL habit wash-hands first; finish, eat, up-to-now. Also, food buy, bring home, wash must; finish, eat can. Plus, other traditions (on fingers); example, cup, bowl, cook pot (cl), wash must. So, Pharisees, they question Jesus: "Tradition your disciples follow not. They go-ahead eat, wash-hands first not, why?" Jesus said, "You hypocrites, Isaiah story right, quote, 'Those people preach honor God, but their heart miss-the-point. Their worship worthless, why? Human law they cherish, God his law ignore.'"

Jesus summon people, announce, "Pay-attention me; try understand. Many things you put-in-mouth++, dirty nothing! Only what throw-out-from-heart, that-one dirty. Warn you. Bad actions start where? Deep heart, dwell-on intercourse, steal, kill, adultery, greed, hurt++, lie, jealous, curse, arrogant, spirit stubborn—#ALL-these (on fingers) start in heart, express, cause 'dirty' [means sin]."

Gospel his Lord.

Twenty-Third Sunday in Ordinary Time

BOOK OF THE PROPHET ISAIAH (35:4–7)

People their heart afraid, tell-them, quote, "Become strong, afraid none! Your God here. He come, ready defeat, save you. Finish, people blind, see will; people deaf, hear; people crippled, run same deer; people can't talk, sing will. Land dry, will water spring~flow. Hot soil become p<u>ond</u> (water~area), water plenty."

Word his Lord.

RESPONSORIAL PSALM (146:7, 8–9, 9–10)

My soul praise Lord.

God himself faithful forever / people oppressed, he judge-fair
Hungry, he give-them food / prison, he give-them out free.

Blind, Lord give-them see / weak, he give-them strong
People good, Lord love / know~new~person, God protect.

No husband? No father? God support / but people bad, he mess-up
Lord control forever / your God forever, alleluia!

LETTER OF JAMES (2:1–5)

My brother~sister, you believe Lord Jesus Christ himself now full glory; means you prefer one person more-than other, better not. Suppose you meeting; wrong, man show-up, himself dressed ritzy, gold rings-on-fingers. Same~time, show-up man poor, dressed worn-out. Suppose you tell-him (rich) "Come, sit here," but tell-him (poor), "You stand," or "Sit down-there." You become judge, but your decision #NG. Hey! Remember, people poor God choose++ for-for? Give-them faith excessive, plus they connect his kingdom can, same he promise #ALL people they love him, connect can.

Word his Lord.

GOSPEL ACCLAMATION

Alleluia

Jesus inform about God kingdom,
People sick, he give them heal.

HOLY GOSPEL ACCORDING TO MARK (7:31–37)

Jesus travel-to Sea of Galilee, area name, quote, Ten Cities [Decapolis]. People few bring man deaf, speak can't, beg Jesus touch, heal. Jesus, two-of-them walk away (cl:1,1), people leave-behind. Jesus touch-ears, spit-on-hand, touch-man's-tongue. Finish, look-up, cry-out, "Ephphatha!" means, "Open!" Quick, man hear, speak clear can. Jesus tell-them people recent happen announce not, but they stubborn announce. They shock. "Expert he! Deaf, he cause hear, speak."

Gospel his Lord.

Twenty-Fourth Sunday in Ordinary Time

BOOK OF THE PROPHET ISAIAH (50:5–9a)

Lord God help-me pay-attention-him; I resist not, ignore not. People beat me, I patient accept; they pluck-beard mine, I offer more; they spit-on-me, I shield-face not. Lord God help-me, I embarrassed not. I stand-strong, know-that I ashamed not. He near; my rights he support. Someone oppose me? Someone my rights against? Come-here, face-to-face. See, Lord God help-me. Who prove me wrong, who?

Word his Lord.

RESPONSORIAL PSALM (116:1–2, 3–4, 5–6, 8–9)

I walk united Lord, now during I live.

Lord I love, my prayer he pay-attention / my cry-out he answer
Happen I summon him / he pay-attention me.

Myself approach die; hell itself summon me; / I become afraid, sad, Lord I cry-out, quote, / "Lord! My life please save!"

Lord himself kind, fair; / true, our God full mercy.
Lord he care for people humble / myself backslide, but he save me.

My soul almost die, but he save me / my tears wipe-away, right way he lead.
I walk united Lord, / now, during my life.

LETTER OF JAMES (2:14–18)

My brother~sister, suppose you talk faith, but action nothing, that worthless. Save you, impossible. Suppose brother, sister have clothes none, food none. You tell-him, "Good <u>luck</u>. Keep yourself warm and eat well," but give-him nothing, worthless. Same-as faith itself #do-do nothing—dead. Maybe you have faith, but I have action, right?

Action dismiss, faith show how? I show faith—how? Action, understand, faith behind.

Word his Lord.

GOSPEL ACCLAMATION

Alleluia

Myself boast what? Our Lord, his cross only
Why? It cross means myself now dead, world I disconnect.

HOLY GOSPEL ACCORDING TO MARK (8:27–35)

Jesus with disciples group-go. Jesus question-them, "People there, they name-me what?" Disciples answer, "Few name-you John Baptizer; other few name-you Elijah; other few name-you prophet." (Jesus) "You? You name-me what?" Peter answer, "Yourself true-work Christ." (Jesus) "Secret. Announce not." Jesus start teach-them what? Himself must suffer these-things (on fingers): (1) suffer; (2) church leader reject, hate; (3) kill-him, die; (4) 3-days later resurrect live again. He explain straight-out. Peter disgruntled, tap-on-shoulder, beckon. Two-of-them (cl:1,1) walk-away, discuss, argue. Jesus look-at-him, "Finish! You devil, away! You think same man, but God think different!" Now Jesus summon people, tell-them, "Any person want connect-to-me, patient accept suffer must. Suppose life you cherish, die will; but suppose die you willing for follow me, safe!"

Gospel his Lord.

Twenty-Fifth Sunday in Ordinary Time

BOOK OF WISDOM (2:12, 17–20)

People bad say, quote, "That man good, we trick-him, why~not? Disgruntle me; our actions, he oppose; our sin, he criticize; our wrong, he blame-me. He speak honest, let's-see. What happen, let's-see. Suppose he true God his son, God defend-him will. Enemy, God protect him. We hate-him, persecute-him, he still gentle, patient, let's-see. Punish him, force-him awful die will we. He say God will care-for him, let's-see."

Word his Lord.

RESPONSORIAL PSALM (54:3–4, 5, 6–8)

My life, Lord himself protect.

God, your name save me / your power protect me
God, my prayer pay-attention-me / my sign-ASL, answer-me.

People arrogant, proud / they oppose-me
They wish kill-me / God they honor not.

God himself help-me / my life, Lord protect.
Sacrifice I willing give-you / your name I praise.

LETTER OF JAMES (3:16—4:3)

Suppose there (l) have jealous, conflict; same there have sin and bad action various. But, there (r) have wise from heaven, same there have innocent, peace, kind, sweet, mercy, and good action. Suppose person encourage peace, God judge-him right will.

You conflict++, argue, for-for? Inside (heart) you want++, can't get, decide kill, take. You jealous, cause-you argue, clash. You want, can't get, why? You ask not-yet. #OR you ask but none, why? You wrong intention. Your goal greedy, self.

Word his Lord.

GOSPEL ACCLAMATION

Alleluia

God summon-us, how? Gospel.
Glory same Lord Jesus Christ he give-us.

HOLY GOSPEL ACCORDING TO MARK (9:30–37)

Jesus with disciples travel through <u>Galilee</u>, secret. Jesus teach disciples, quote, "Future, someone hand-me-over, those men kill-me. Three-days later, I resurrect live again." Apostles understand none, but question-him, afraid. Arrive town name <u>Capernaum</u>, house enter, Jesus ask them, "Recent travel, you discuss what?" They quiet, why? They up-to-now argue apostle most important, which. Jesus sit down, tell them, "Any person become move-to-thumb first want, willing become move-to-last, serve #ALL must he." Finish, child, Jesus put-him-in-front, said, "Any person serve child willing, that person accept me same. Suppose you accept serve me, means God himself you accept."

Gospel his Lord.

Twenty-Sixth Sunday in Ordinary Time

BOOK OF NUMBERS (11:25–29)

Cloud, God there, talk-to Moses. Finish, spirit inspire Moses; some spirit God take, share 70 Israel leaders. Happen spirit touch++, they start predict.

Two men [name <u>Eldad</u> and <u>Medad</u>], two-of-them not there meeting, stay camp. Their name, list, go-to meeting should, but two-of-them stay camp. Holy spirit touch them, they start predict same. Young man tell Moses, "Those-two predict there camp." <u>Joshua</u> upset, said, "Tell-them stop." Moses answer, "Jealous you? I wish #ALL people predict can. I wish #ALL people God spirit touch."

Word his Lord.

RESPONSORIAL PSALM (19:8, 10, 12–13, 14)

Lord his law give-us heart happy.

Lord his law perfect / our soul inspire
Lord his decide, we trust can / people humble become wise.

Honor Lord true / continue forever, ever;
Lord his law true / #ALL (down fingers) fair.

God law I study, learn / obey give-me happy
Suppose I sin, know-nothing, overlook / please God forgive me.

Myself plan, intend sin, no! / Allow sin control me not.
Help-me live right / awful sin, I innocent.

LETTER OF JAMES (5:1–6)

You people rich, cry should you, why? Near-future trouble. Your money wear-out, your fine clothes ruined, your gold dissolve. Your wealth cause-you sin, destroy-you compare fire. Why? Money you store-up for yourselves for future last day, but here farm workers cry-out for money, you pay-them refuse. Their complaint, God finish hear. You live comfortable, you become fat, compare cow ready for kill-eat. Innocent man, you punish, kill; he patient, accept.

Word his Lord.

GOSPEL ACCLAMATION

Alleluia

Lord, your word itself honest,
Please your honest inspire us.

HOLY GOSPEL ACCORDING TO MARK (9:38–43, 45, 47–48)

<u>John</u> tell Jesus, "Teacher, we see man he use your name for devil eliminate. We try stop-him, why? our group he connect not." Jesus answer, "Stop him, no-wave. Any person use my name, action wonderful work, he talk bad about me can't, impossible. Any person himself not opposite-me, that-one connect-me. Suppose person give-you water drink because you connect me, I promise, bless-him will I. But, suppose innocent believer, that person lead-him wrong way, better rock tied-around-neck (cl), ocean toss-into, drown.

"Suppose your hand cause-you sin, cut-it-off. Have one hand touch heaven (r), two hands touch hell (l), it (one hand—r) better. Suppose your foot cause-you sin, cut-it-off. Crippled touch heaven (r), both feet touch hell (l), it better (one foot—r). Suppose your eye cause-you sin, tear-it-out. Have one eye touch heaven, two eyes touch hell, it (one eye) better—why? There hell, awful, worm die never, fire dissolve never."

Gospel his Lord.

Twenty-Seventh Sunday in Ordinary Time

BOOK OF GENESIS (2:18–24)

Lord God said, "Man live alone, not good. Make appropriate partner will I." So, Lord God make animals, birds, various, show-to man, let's-see he name-them what. Name decide, stay. #ALL animal, bird, man name++; but appropriate partner none. Lord God cause-him sleep-hard, <u>rib</u> take, close-up. <u>Rib</u>, God make become woman. Man wake-up, God show-him woman, he (man) say, "Succeed, this (hon) body same-as-me. I name-her 'woman'—why? She come (cl: c against side, s take-out) from man." Now man mother~father depart, wife connect, two-of-them become one body.

Word his Lord.

RESPONSORIAL PSALM (128:1–2, 3, 4–5, 6)

Lord please bless us during life from-now-on.

#IF Lord you honor, his wants follow, bless you.

#IF Lord you honor, his want follow / bless you will he
Your work succeed, you benefit / God bless you, cherish you

Your wife many children born +++ / there your home
Your children grow++ / table they sit-around (cl:crooked v, v)

Suppose Lord you honor / God bless you same
There heaven, Lord see, bless
Hope see Jerusalem succeed / during your life, forever.

I hope you see your children generations-forward.
Peace touch Israel!

LETTER OF PAUL TO THE HEBREWS (2:9–11)

Jesus allow himself demote than angels—why? Die for save #ALL people he want. Strange, God powerful! make everything, but Jesus, God cause-him suffer++, become perfect; finish, #ALL people he bring-up touch glory. Now Jesus himself bless us, why? two-of-us have same Father. Means what? He name-us brother his—ashamed not he.

Word his Lord.

GOSPEL ACCLAMATION

Alleluia

Suppose we love each-other, God socialize-with us
His love become perfect in us.

HOLY GOSPEL ACCORDING TO MARK (10:2–16)

Pharisee few try test Jesus, question-him, "Husband, wife divorce can?" Jesus tell-them, "Moses command what?" (Pharisees) "Divorce, Moses permit." Jesus inform-them, "Yes, because you people stubborn. But long-ago beginning God make man, woman. Father, mother man depart must, wife two-of-them become one body. Not two, one. God finish put-together connect; people decide disconnect, prohibit." Later, disciples question-him more. Jesus explain, "Suppose husband, wife divorce, he marry-left, she marry-right, adultery they."

People bring children, want Jesus touch-them. Apostles bawl-them-out, get-away. But Jesus notice, disgruntled, tell-them, "Children bring, prevent not. They connect heaven. Any person accept heaven same children, he heaven succeed." Finish, Jesus hug (children), bless, lay-on-hands.

Gospel his Lord.

Twenty-Eighth Sunday in Ordinary Time

BOOK OF WISDOM (7:7–11)

I pray, finish, God give-me wise; I beg, finish, wise come-to-me (cl:1). Wise, I cherish—more-than (1) throne, (2) money, (3) valuable diamond. Wise (r), gold (l) compare, it (gold) worthless, silver (l) trivial. Wise I love more-than health, more-than beauty. Wise (r), light (l), I choose it (r—wisdom)—why? It "light-go-out" never. But wise give-me everything good. All-these (l—on fingers), wise give-me.

Word his Lord.

RESPONSORIAL PSALM (90:12–13, 14–15, 16–17)

Your love fill-me-up, Lord, sing happy will we.

Lord, teach-us count our days, see life whew short / finish, wise will we
Come, Lord! We wait, how long? / We your servant, mercy-us.

Morning, your kindness fill-me-up / we shout happy, celebrate forever
Long-ago, you punish-us, but now happy / many years we suffer,
but now celebrate.

Please allow us your work see / our children your glory see
Please Lord God himself care-for us / Give our work succeed!
Give our work succeed!

LETTER TO THE HEBREWS (4:12–13)

God his word expert, sharp more-than sword. Our soul, our action, his word analyze. Our thoughts, his word judge. We hide nothing, everything open, our sin he see, we explain must.

Word his Lord.

GOSPEL ACCLAMATION

Alleluia

People their spirit depend-on God, bless them
Kingdom heaven connect-to them.

HOLY GOSPEL ACCORDING TO MARK (10:17–30)

Jesus walk (cl:1), wrong, man approach-him (cl:1), kneel-down, question-him, "Good Teacher, live forever I want, #do-do me?" Jesus answer, "You name-me good, why? Only God himself good. You know commandments: (1) kill not, (2) adultery not, (3) steal not, (4) lie not, (5) knock not, mother~father honor." Man say, "These-things (on fingers) I finish obey up-to-now grow-up." Jesus look-at-him, love, said, "One~more must you. Everything you have, sell, money get, give-to poor. Finish, you rich there heaven. Sell finish, come follow me." Man depressed, why? Himself have many things, cherish.

Jesus tell disciples, "Rich man touch heaven, whew, difficult!" They puzzled. Jesus again said, "Touch heaven, whew, difficult. <u>Camel</u> through <u>needle</u>, rich man touch heaven, it (camel) easier." Apostles shock, discuss-among-themselves, "Save, how possible?" Jesus look-at-them, said, "Man save himself, impossible, but for God, everything possible." <u>Peter</u> touch-heart, said, "Everything we push-aside, follow you." Jesus tell-him, "I promise, suppose any person his home, brother, sister, mother, father, children, property give-up for me and for gospel, he receive now time-period 100 more home, brother, sister, mother, children, property—also persecution—plus, future he live forever."

Gospel his Lord.

Twenty-Ninth Sunday in Ordinary Time

BOOK OF THE PROPHET ISAIAH (53:10–11)

He servant, God himself decide destroy. Suppose he (servant) die for sin willing, descendents many will he, and God his plan succeed will. Because he suffer, he future touch heaven. Through suffer, my servant will cause many people connect-with God; their sin, their punish he accept.

Word his Lord.

RESPONSORIAL PSALM (33:4–5, 18–19, 20, 22)

Lord, please mercy-us. You we trust.

Lord his word right / his work we trust.
Judge~fair, honest, he cherish / Lord his kindness spread-over earth.

People they honor Lord, hope for his kindness / he care-for-them.
Die, he save them / food none, he fill-up them.

Our soul wait-for Lord / himself help, protect.
Lord, please mercy-us. You we trust.

LETTER TO THE HEBREWS (4:14–16)

Brother~sister, we have priest~most himself finish touch heaven— who? Jesus, son [of] God. Please trust Jesus continue. Our weakness, priest~most he understand; temptation he experience every kind same-as-us, but sin none. Now, go-ahead, confident, face-to-face God and pray, receive mercy, love, and help time need.

Word his Lord.

GOSPEL ACCLAMATION

Alleluia

God his son come-down (cl:1) for serve,
Die for save many.

HOLY GOSPEL ACCORDING TO MARK (10:35–45)

<u>Zebedee</u> have son two: (1) <u>James</u>, (2) <u>John</u>. Two-of-them come-to (cl:v) Jesus, tell-him, "Teacher, we want something." (Jesus) "What?" (James and John) "Happen you succeed glory, we-two want sit with-you, right, left." Jesus tell-them, "You ask, but understand not-yet. You drink cup same-as-me, suffer same-as-me can you? (James and John) "We can." (Jesus) "You drink cup same-as-me will; you suffer same-as-me will, but two-of-you sit right, left, I promise can't. It-right, it-left reserve for someone, I don't-know who." Other apostles ten hear those-three story, disgruntled they. Jesus summon "Come-here," said, "You know-that those non-Jews, they tend oppress++. Their leader want full control, strict. You different. Become important want? Serve must. Become first want? Slave must you, serve #ALL. Myself come-down (cl:1) for-for? You serve me? No, I serve you, die for save many."

Gospel his Lord.

Thirtieth Sunday in Ordinary Time

BOOK OF THE PROPHET JEREMIAH (31:7–9)

Lord says, Shout happy, celebrate, announce praise, say, quote, "Lord succeed save his people Israel." See, from north, from all-over world, I bring-them, no-matter blind, crippled, pregnant. They flock-to-here. Long-ago, they depart crying, but now I mercy-them, lead-them [to] water~flowing, road smooth, none trip-fall-down. I myself their father, they compare my first~born son.

Word his Lord.

RESPONSORIAL PSALM (126:1–2, 2–3, 4–5, 6)

Actions wonderful Lord succeed, inspire happy we.

Long-ago Israel people slavery, God save us / feel compare dream
We happy, laugh, / sing, sign-ASL, celebrate.

People other country said, / "Actions wonderful, Lord succeed for them"
True~work, Lord wonderful action for us / happy true we.

Lord, please give-us bless / compare desert, you-give-it rain
People they work, grieve / they succeed happy will.

They go-out crying / sack it have <u>seed</u> for scatter
Future come home happy / <u>wheat</u> carry-in-arms.

LETTER TO THE HEBREWS (5:1–6)

Every priest~most, God choose special stand face-to-face God, pray, offer~sacrifice for those people their sin. Priest patient care-for sinner can, why? Himself weak same-as-sinner, means he sacrifice for himself also. ? Mean person himself decide become priest? No, God choose, same long-ago <u>Aaron</u> God choose. Christ himself take-up glory, decide become priest~most? No. Jesus patient, wait for God say, "You my son, today I choose-you" also "You priest forever, same long-ago Melchizedek."

Word his Lord.

GOSPEL ACCLAMATION

Alleluia

Die, Lord Jesus Christ destroy-it
Life give how? Gospel preach.

HOLY GOSPEL ACCORDING TO MARK (10:46–52)

Town name Jericho, Jesus ready leave with disciples, happen blind man sit there, his name Bartimaeus. He hear rumor that-one Jesus, he call-out, "Jesus, Son [of] David, mercy-me." People tell-him quiet, but he stubborn shout-out loud, "Son [of] David, mercy-me." Jesus stop, say, "Tell-him come-here." People tell-him, "Jesus summon you. Fear none. Go-to-it." Man jump-up, run-to-Jesus (cl:1). (Jesus) "You want what?" (Bartimaeus) "I want see." (Jesus) "Oh-I-see. Away. Your faith cause-you heal." Quick, man see can, Jesus follow.

Gospel his Lord.

Thirty-First Sunday in Ordinary Time

BOOK OF DEUTERONOMY (6:2–6)

Moses tell people: "Honor Lord your God, #ALL his laws and commandments I recent inform-you obey, long life will you. Israel people, pay-attention-to-me; these laws obey. Finish, you succeed fine! God long-ago promise, he give you what? Land, milk and honey overflow. Pay-attention-to-me, Israel people. Lord only true our God. You love Lord your God with full heart, full soul, full strong must you. I preach, you learn-lesson."

Word his Lord.

RESPONSORIAL PSALM (18:2–3, 3–4, 47, 51)

Lord, I love you, honor-you.

Lord, I love you, honor-you / yourself my support, my defend, my protect.

My God, my mighty protector / my savior, my defender, care-er
Praise Lord, sign-ASL-to-him / my enemies, he save-me.

Lord live forever. Praise my support / honor God my savior
Your king, you give-him success / person you choose,
you give-him kind.

LETTER TO THE HEBREWS (7:23–28)

Past, Old Testament, have priest many—why? Priest die, new priest replace. But Jesus live forever—he continue priest forever. People themselves follow Jesus, they go face-to-face God, Jesus save them—how? He always live, ready help them.

Jesus, he right priest~most for us—why? He holy, innocent, sin~none; sinners he separate-from; himself heaven exceed. Other priest sacrifice every-day must, first for his #OWN sin, then for sin theirs people. Jesus different. He sacrifice himself once finish, again not~need. Law establish priest himself man—weak. But God choose his Son become priest~most—why? His son perfect forever.

Word his Lord.

GOSPEL ACCLAMATION

Alleluia

Lord say, "Any person love me, my order he obey.
Finish, my father love him, two-of-us meet-him. (cl:2,1)"

HOLY GOSPEL ACCORDING TO MARK (12:28–34)

Happen one scribe meet Jesus, question-to-him, "Which commandment most important?" Jesus tell-him, "First (on index finger), quote, 'Pay-attention-me, Israel! Lord your God, himself Lord only! Love Lord your God with full heart, soul, mind, strong must you.' First. Second (on middle finger), quote, 'You love yourself, other people love same must you.' Those-two most important." (Scribe) "Good answer. You say God himself only, have none other, you right. Love him with full heart, mind, strong, first; second, love other people same-as-me myself—those two worth! than fire~sacrifice." Jesus oh-I-see, wise man he. Tell-him, "Kingdom his God, you near." From-then-on, no person brave question-him (Jesus).

Gospel his Lord.

Thirty-Second Sunday in Ordinary Time

FIRST BOOK OF KINGS (17:10–16)

City name <u>Zarephath</u>, <u>Elijah</u> go-to. Arrive, notice woman, husband dead, she gather wood for fire. Tell-her, "Please bring-me water drink." Woman "OK," walk-away (cl:1) He "Hey! Bread same-same, please!" Woman said, "Inform-you honest, I have none bread. Jar (cl), <u>flour</u> one-inch (cl:g), oil little-bit have. Now wood I collect, bring home, last food cook. Finish, son two-of-us die." (Elijah) "Worry not. Go home. First, bread make, bring-me. Finish, food cook for yourself and son can you. Lord, himself God [of] Israel, he says, '<u>Flour</u> use-up not, oil run-out not, until day Lord cause rain-on earth.'" Woman go, action same <u>Elijah</u> tell-her. Happen, woman, son, <u>Elijah</u>, three-of-them, have food plenty for one year. <u>Flour</u> use-up not; oil run-out not, same Lord promise through <u>Elijah</u>.

Word his Lord.

RESPONSORIAL PSALM (146:6–7, 8–9, 9–10)

My soul praise Lord

Lord he faithful forever / people oppressed give-them judge~fair,
People hungry, he feed / slave, Lord give-them free

People blind, Lord give-them see / oppressed, he raise-them
People honest. Lord love / know~new~person, he protect.

Parents none? Husband none? God support / person bad, he punish.
Lord, he control forever / your God, forever ever.

LETTER TO THE HEBREWS (9:24–28)

Christ enter holy place—who make? Holy place people make, try copy heaven? No, Christ enter heaven face-to-face God, pray for us.

Understand, here earth, temple, priest~most enter every-year, animal blood sacrifice must. Christ sacrifice himself again, again, not~need. Jesus come once, sacrifice himself for sin remove; again not~need. Know-that every person die once, finish, face-to-face judge. Christ same. Die once for many people their sin remove. Again come will; again sin remove? Wave-no, those people enthusiastic wait, he save.

GOSPEL ACCLAMATION

Alleluia

Bless those people they depend-on God
Kingdom heaven connect-to them.

HOLY GOSPEL ACCORDING TO MARK (12:38–44)

Jesus teach: "Warn, careful those <u>scribes</u>—why? They big-head, like clothes ritzy. Out walk, they want people honor, bow-down-to-them. Church, they want best seat front. Feast, they want important place sit. <u>Widow</u>, she money save, they take. Finish, they pray exaggerate, want people look (cl:ff), whew! Impress! God punish them worse! will."

Jesus sit, watch, people flock-to church, money put-in++. Few rich, big-cash (cl:c) put-in. Wrong, <u>widow</u> poor walk-to (cl:1), coins (cl:f) two put-in, worth how-much? One-cent. Jesus tell disciples, "Notice woman poor? She give more than #ALL other—why? They have plenty, some give. She have tiny-bit, whole-thing give."

Gospel his Lord.

Thirty-Third Sunday in Ordinary Time

BOOK OF THE PROPHET DANIEL (12:1–3)

<u>Daniel</u>, God tell-him: Future happen, <u>Michael</u>, himself strong prince, he show-up, your people care-for. Future time-period, happen awful trouble never past up-to-now. Many people escape will—who? People their name book jot-down. Many people finish dead, buried, they wake-up, resurrect will. Some go (up) forever live, some go (down) forever shame, suffer. People wise will shine, sun same. People themselves teach other people live right, they shine, stars same.

Word his Lord.

RESPONSORIAL PSALM (16:5, 8, 9–10, 11)

Lord, only-you I depend-on.

Lord, I cherish-you / my future, you lead, protect
Lord I follow always / God accompany, I afraid nothing.

My heart happy, my soul celebrate / my body laid-back, confident
I know-that my soul God abandon never / my body he care-for, ruin never.

Way [to] heaven, you show-me / happy with you, will I
Enjoy socialize together / forever, ever.

LETTER TO THE HEBREWS (10:11–14, 18)

Every-day, priest pray sacrifice monotonous; sin forgive can't. But Jesus sacrifice himself once for sin forgive; finish, stay forever with God. Now Jesus wait—for-for? Time enemy beat (shot-h). Christ sacrifice himself once, cause his people perfect forever. Sin forgive once finish, more sacrifice not~need.

Word his Lord.

GOSPEL ACCLAMATION

Alleluia

Pay-attention, ready always,
Pray become strong happen Son of God face-to-face.

HOLY GOSPEL ACCORDING TO MARK (13:24–32)

Jesus tell disciples, "Future happen trouble various; finish, sun light-go-out, moon blow-on-hand, stars twinkle-fall, sky everything mess-up. Finish, son <u>of</u> God come (cl:1) full power, glory, people see will. Angels he send all-around world, his people from all-over earth collect. Notice <u>fig</u> tree, learn lesson. Happen <u>sap</u>, wet, flow-up-trunk, sprout++, you know near-future summer. Compare same, happen you see these-things (on fingers) I recent tell-you, know-that son <u>of</u> God near-future come. I promise, these-things (on fingers) will happen during time-period you-all people still live. Heaven and earth dissolve will, but my word dissolve never. Exact day, hour—don't-know. Angels there heaven don't-know; I don't-know. Father himself knows."

Gospel his Lord.

CHRIST THE KING

BOOK OF THE PROPHET DANIEL (7:13–14)

All-night, <u>Daniel</u> envision: there cloud (left), person face~same man come (cl:1, lh, left-to-right), face-to-face God. Power, glory, full control, God give-him. #ALL country, people every language serve him; his control continue forever; defeat-him never, destroy never.

Word his Lord.

RESPONSORIAL PSALM (93:1, 1–2, 5)

Lord himself king, glory he (hon).

Lord true~work king, glory he (hon) / Lord himself full mighty
World he make, stand-strong / vibrate, collapse never

God his control up-to-now mighty / himself live since forever.
God his law good, right / his home holy / forever, ever.

BOOK OF REVELATION (1:5–8)

Jesus Christ true faithful witness. Many people die, Jesus first resurrect. King strong control here earth, Jesus worse. He loves us, our sin remove, how? His blood. He cause us become priest++, for serve God father. Glory, honor give-him forever, ever. Amen (in palm)! See, cloud he come (cl:1). Every person see-him will, those finish kill-him, they see-him will. #ALL people here earth cry, grieve for him. True happen will! Amen (in palm)!

Lord God say, quote, "Myself first, last. I up-to-now, forever almighty God."

Word his Lord.

GOSPEL ACCLAMATION

Alleluia

Honor him, he come name Lord
Honor him, <u>David</u> he descend, his kingdom control forever.

HOLY GOSPEL ACCORDING TO JOHN (18:33–37)

<u>Pilate</u> question-to Jesus, "?? Yourself king theirs Jews?" Jesus answer, "You, self interested, or other people story about me, which?" (Pilate) "Jew nothing me! Your people, your priest~most put-you-here. Wrong #do-do you?" (Jesus) "My kingdom here earth not. Suppose my kingdom here, my people willing fight save me, put-me-there Jews, refuse. But my kingdom not here." (Pilate) "Oh-I-see. Mean you true~work king?" (Jesus) "You name-me king. I born here world for-for? Teach honest. Any person himself honest enthusiastic, my teach he pay-attention."

Gospel his Lord.

Presentation of the Lord

BOOK OF MALACHI (3:1–4)

Lord God say, quote, "See, my informer I send, he prepare way for me." Finish, happen what? Lord, that-one you wait-for up-to-now, he come-down (cl:1), temple touch, new promise bring. Yes, he come near-future.

But day he come, who can tolerate (patient)? He show-up, who brave, who? He compare fire, silver put-in, fire++, pah! Pure, perfect, ready. Priest, he cause-them pure same silver, why? They clean, kill~sacrifice-to Lord can. Now, Jerusalem, its sacrifice God see, satisfied, same long-ago God satisfied.

Word his Lord.

RESPONSORIAL PSALM (24:7, 8, 9, 10)

King glory, who? Lord himself!

You gates, open-out, open-up, / King glory enter
King glory, who? Lord, himself strong, mighty / Lord himself war defeat

You gates, open-out open-up, / King glory enter
King glory, who? Lord, he control heaven / himself King glory.

LETTER TO THE HEBREWS (2:14–18)

People have body, blood; same Jesus have body, blood. Himself willing die, why? Devil destroy; give us free. Now die, we afraid? No!

Angels, Jesus help-them not, but Jew people, he help-them. Means Jesus become full human must. Why? He become same priest~most, faithful, mercy-them, pray-to God please their sin forgive. Jesus himself finish suffer; now people suffer, he understand, help-them can.

Word his Lord.

GOSPEL ACCLAMATION

Alleluia

Light for not~Jew and glory for Jew people.

HOLY GOSPEL ACCORDING TO LUKE (2:22–40)

Law Moses, Mary, Joseph follow, baby Jesus bring-to Jerusalem, for-for? Offer-to God. Law require what? Every first-born boy offer-to-Lord must. Plus, parents sacrifice birds two must, follow law. Happen there Jerusalem man name Simeon, himself good, holy, he wait-for Messiah arrive. Holy Spirit inform-him what? He live, see Messiah; finish, die. Now, Holy Spirit tell-him temple go-to, see Mary, Joseph, Jesus. Baby, he (Simeon) take-in-arms, praise God, said, "Now die peace can I, why? Your promise satisfied. Savior you send for #ALL people, light for non-Jews and glory for Jew people, I finish see."

Mary, Joseph listen, puzzled. Two-of-them Simeon bless, tell Mary, "This baby will grow-up, cause many people fail and many people succeed all-over Israel. People oppose-him will; and yourself suffer, for-for? People their thought++ show clear."

There temple have woman prophet name Anna, herself old. Long-ago she married, live with husband 7 years, he die; she live alone up-to-now, now age 84. She frequented temple, all-day, all-night worship, fasting, pray. Now arrive, baby see, thank God; finish, she inform-all Jesus save Jerusalem will.

Law obey finish, family group-go #BACK home Nazareth. Baby grow-up, strong, wise; God his grace influence-him.

Gospel his Lord.

NATIVITY OF JOHN THE BAPTIST

BOOK OF THE PROPHET ISAIAH (49:1–6)

#ALL people, far-away, pay-attention-me—Israel speak! Happen I establish not-yet, Lord finish summon-me, my name call-out. Preach tough he give-me, compare sword sharp, but stab not-yet. He tell-me, "You my servant, Israel. My glory you show." Israel work, try, worthless. But God see, he praise will. Lord, himself finish make Israel, for-for? #ALL Jew people summon, come-here Israel, worship Lord. Finish, Israel become glory, strong. Now, Lord tell-me, "You serve God, #ALL Jew people summon, come-here Israel—trivial! I give-you more—now Israel important compare light for #ALL countries, inform-them what? God save-them."

Word his Lord.

RESPONSORIAL PSALM (139:1–3, 13–14, 14–15)

I praise you because you wonderful make me.

Lord, you analyze-me, know me / happen I sit, stand, you notice
My thoughts, you finish know /
Suppose I travel, [or] stop, rest, you see / my tendencies (on fingers) you understand.

My body, soul you make / in my mother pregnant, you make++
I thank you, why? You wonderful make me / everything (out there) you make wonderful.

My soul you know full / my body you know full same
Secret, you make me / my body you invent, build.

ACTS OF THE APOSTLES (13:22–26)

<u>Paul</u> preach, quote, "Long-ago, God choose <u>David</u> become king, why? <u>David</u> himself good man, obey God. <u>David</u> generations-down, born savior name Jesus. <u>John</u> Baptist, he preach, inform people now life change must. Finish, he tell-them, 'Myself savior, think you? No, not me, but near-future other man come, his shoes touch, I not worth enough.' Means what? You Jew, not~Jew, no-matter. God promise save-you!"

Word his Lord.

GOSPEL ACCLAMATION

Alleluia

People will name-you, quote, "God his prophet."
Why? You travel, preach, prepare for God come-down.

HOLY GOSPEL ACCORDING TO LUKE (1:57–66, 80)

<u>Elizabeth</u> pregnant, time, born son. Her friends, family happy celebrate. Eight-days later, time for circumcise and name give-him, family think name-him <u>Zechariah</u>, same father. But <u>Elizabeth</u> said, "No. Name <u>John</u>." Understand, family none name <u>John</u>. Family question-to father, <u>Zechariah</u>, baby name-him what? Father talk can't, ask-for paper, write, quote, "Baby name <u>John</u>." Quick, talk again can! He happy, praise God.

Family, friends afraid, gossip spread all-over <u>Judea</u>. People wonder, that baby grow-up, #do-do? Seem God choose-him special. Baby, he grow-up, become strong spirit, live there desert until time begin preach Israel.

Gospel his Lord.

Saints Peter and Paul, Apostles

ACTS OF THE APOSTLES (12:1–11)

Members Christian church, king hate them. James, king order sword~stab. Jews few happy; king see, decide Peter arrest. During celebrate Passover, king order Peter arrest, throw-in jail, soldiers guard. King plan wait Passover finish, Peter bring face-to-face people. Peter stuck jail; Christians pray God protect him. Night, tomorrow court, Peter sleep, chains-on-wrists, soldiers watch-him; wrong happen angel appear, light-shine-from-him. Peter, angel tap-on-shoulder, wake up. Shackles-fall-off-wrists; angel tell-him, "Shoes put-on, belt-put-on; cloak-put-on, follow me." Peter follow, how angel cause happen++, understand not. Seem dream. Two-of-them walk (cl:v) past soldier, arrive gate, itself open. Two-of-them walk (cl:v) narrow street; wrong, angel depart. [Peter now think clear, understand, oh-I-see, angel Lord send for save him. Now king and Jews kill-him can't.]

Word his Lord.

RESPONSORIAL PSALM (34:2–3, 4–5, 6–7, 8–9)

Honor Lord, his angel save-you will.

I honor Lord always / his praise I sign-ASL
My soul have glory with Lord / people humble see, celebrate.

Two-of-us glory give-to Lord / together his name we praise
Past I depend-on Lord, he answer-me / my fear, he remove.

Look-at God, you happy, radiant-face will / you blush, ashamed never
Happen you cry-out-to God, he pay-attention / trouble he save-you

Lord his angel protect you, save you / understand, you honor him
Taste, see, Lord himself good / man trust him (God), he bless.

SECOND LETTER OF PAUL TO TIMOTHY (4:6–8, 17–18)

I approach time die. I up-to-now stubborn continue; race I finish; faith I cherish. Now crown God have for me. Lord judge me, crown-me—not only me, same-same #ALL people themselves enthusiastic wait-for him come. Lord up-to-now support-me, give-me strong, I preach gospel country there++, can I. God save me, lion consume-me, he not allow. He continue protect-me until heaven I arrive safe. Glory give-him forever, ever.

Word his Lord.

GOSPEL ACCLAMATION

Alleluia

Your name <u>Peter</u>; this rock, my church I establish
Devil destroy never.

HOLY GOSPEL ACCORDING TO MATTHEW (16:13–19)

Apostles, Jesus question-to-them, ? "Those people name-me what?" They tell-him, "Some name-you <u>John</u> Baptizer, other name-you <u>Jeremiah</u> or other prophet." (Jesus) "You name-me what?" <u>Simon Peter</u> say, "Yourself true Messiah, son his God." Jesus tell-him, "Bless you, <u>Simon</u>. God himself tell-you true who I (hon). Inform-you, your name <u>Rock</u>; on this rock my church I establish, itself die never. Key for heaven kingdom I give-you. Suppose you decide something bound here earth, there heaven I agree, support. Suppose you decide something free here earth, there heaven I agree free."

Gospel his Lord.

TRANSFIGURATION OF THE LORD

BOOK OF THE PROPHET DANIEL (7:9–10, 13–14)

I envision see throne (r); God himself sit there. His clothes white! compare snow; hair white. Throne itself fire, have wheels fire, flame-outward. Many, many people serve him, million people audience. Time meeting, quiet, book~open.

Now I see person (l) name son of man, he come (cl:1), face-to-face (God). Control, glory God give-him, become king, he. #ALL people, countries, language serve him (son of man) must. He control forever, break-down never, dissolve never.

Word his Lord.

RESPONSORIAL PSALM (97:1–2, 5–6, 9)

Lord himself king, whole earth he exceed, control.

Lord himself king, #ALL people celebrate / island there++ happy
Cloud, dark, swirl-around him (cl:1,5) / his throne judge fair.

Happen Lord look, mountain break-down, / whole earth,
Lord control
Heaven announce he judge fair / his glory, #ALL people see.

Lord, yourself control all-over earth / other gods, you exceed.

SECOND LETTER OF PETER (1:16–19)

We inform-you honest, invent++ nothing. We story Jesus his power; he come~again will, we know-that, how? We finish see God Father give-him glory, announce, quote, "Here my son, I cherish; satisfied me." There holy mountain, voice from heaven we hear. Plus, myself true~work prophet; my inform, you trust can. Better you pay-attention me, follow; compare place dark, candle see, follow. Later, yourself understand.

Word his Lord.

GOSPEL ACCLAMATION

Alleluia

He (hon) my cherish son, satisfy me.
Pay-attention him.

HOLY GOSPEL ACCORDING TO MARK (9:2–10)

Jesus with Peter, James, and John, four-of-them mountain group-go, pray. Jesus pray, wrong, himself change. Face, clothes become white, wow. Elijah, Moses, show-up there (l), there (r), glory; three-of-them discuss Jesus near-future die there Jerusalem. Peter, three-of-them up-to-now sleep, but now wake-up, see those-three glory. Peter tell Jesus, "Lord, three-of-us see you glory, that good. We build tent three, for you++." True, he know-nothing.

Wrong, cloud over. Apostles afraid. They hear voice say, "He (hon) my cherish son. Pay-attention him." Apostles look-around, see Jesus alone. Three-of-them quiet, announce nothing.

Gospel his Lord.

Assumption of the Blessed Virgin Mary

BOOK OF REVELATION (11:19a, 12:1–6a, 10)

Heaven open, see God his <u>ark</u>. Sky, see woman (center). Herself clothes, sun shine-out-from-her; moon (lh) stand-on; crown, stars, altogether twelve. Woman herself pregnant, cry-out, wring-stomach, ready give-birth. Wrong, show-up (l) what? <u>Dragon</u>, breathe-fire, huge, red, head++ altogether seven, crown++ seven. His <u>tail</u> swish-back-and-forth; stars, swish! 1/3 flutter-to-earth. He stand, wait woman give-birth, plan grab, consume. Woman born son, himself #ALL countries control strict will he. God grab, carry-to throne. Woman escape desert, there God prepare place special for her. Finish, I hear voice loud say: "Now God save succeed, now God control and Jesus muscle succeed."

Word his Lord.

RESPONSORIAL PSALM (45:20, 11, 12, 16)

Queen there with God, clothes gold.

Queen there with God, clothes gold / gold from where? <u>Ophir</u>

Daughter, pay-attention / your father, your family, push aside.

You beautiful, king cherish you / himself your lord.

Two-of-you full happy, celebrate / king his home enter.

FIRST LETTER OF PAUL TO THE CORINTHIANS (15:20–26)

Christ finish die, resurrect; himself first person resurrect live again. One man (l) cause #ALL die, now one man (r) cause #ALL resurrect, live again. <u>Adam</u> cause #ALL die; but Christ cause #ALL live again: first Christ himself, later he come again, his followers #ALL resurrect will. Finish, whole power collapse, destroy, dissolve; kingdom left-there, Christ give-to God Father. Christ control continue must until #ALL enemies God destroy. Last enemy what? <u>Death</u>—beat (shot-h).

Word his Lord.

GOSPEL ACCLAMATION

Alleluia

Mary, God take-up, carry heaven
Angels hordes celebrate, happy.

HOLY GOSPEL ACCORDING TO LUKE (1:39–56)

Town there <u>Judah</u> Mary hurry, arrive, house enter, <u>Elizabeth</u> meet, hug. Happen <u>Elizabeth</u>, she hear Mary voice, her baby move. Holy Spirit inspire (Elizabeth), she cry-out: "Bless you, most high woman! Bless your baby pregnant! Mother his Lord visit me, why? Myself trivial, me. Instant your voice I hear, my baby happy, move. Bless you, why? Lord his promise you trust."

Mary said, "My heart announce Lord himself wonderful; my spirit happy celebrate God, my savior, why? He notice-me (hon), his servant humble. #ALL people future name-me holy. God himself mighty, wonderful things he finish action for me; his name true holy. He mercy continue++ for people—understand, they honor him. His power he show, how? People proud, feel themselves wise, he mess-up. People power, throne, he throw-out; people humble, poor, he put-there (in their place). People hungry, he give-them satisfy, but people rich, he give-them nothing, send-away. He up-to-now support Israel; always he mercy++, same he promise our ancestor Abraham, pass-down++ forever."

Mary stay with <u>Elizabeth</u> three-months; finish, #BACK home.

Gospel his Lord.

Exaltation of the Holy Cross

BOOK OF NUMBERS (21:4–9)

Israel people travel++, patient~suffer, complain Moses, quote, "Awful there Egypt you lead-us here desert die, why? Food, water, none. Food here, we hate!" Those people, Lord punish, how? Send snake many, bite++, cause die. People tell Moses, "We complain, sorry. We sin. Please you pray God snakes remove." Moses pray for people, Lord tell-him, "Yourself make pole (cl:f,f), snake metal put-on-top, stab-in-ground. Any person snake bite, he look (at pole), healed will he." Moses make snake <u>bronze</u>, pole put-on-top, stab-in-ground. Happen snake bite, person look (at pole), healed succeed.

Word his Lord.

RESPONSORIAL PSALM (78:1–2, 34–35, 36–37, 38)

Lord his actions, forget not!

People, my teach pay-attention / my talk, please listen!
Story I tell-you / secret honest, I explain will.

Happen God kill-them, they quick sorry / want follow God again.
They remember, oh-I-see, God true our support /
himself expert save us.

They butter-up (God), they slick-talk / they promise these things
(on fingers) but lie.
Their heart cherish God not / they faithful obey him not.

But God himself full mercy, their sin he forgive / he destroy-them not.
His anger he restrain / he lose-temper not, calm-down.

LETTER OF PAUL TO PHILIPPIANS (2:6–11)

Christ Jesus, himself true God, yes, but he cherish it (point upward) not. No, Jesus willing born same slave. Himself human 100%. He humble obey Father, accept die there cross. Now, God raise-him live again, give-him name #ALL other name exceed. Happen Jesus name hear, every person kneel-down must, there heaven, here earth, there hell, every voice announce, give glory God Father, quote, "Jesus Christ true Lord."

Word his Lord.

GOSPEL ACCLAMATION

Alleluia

Christ, we adore, praise you.
Cross you die, world save.

HOLY GOSPEL ACCORDING TO JOHN (3:13–17)

<u>Nicodemus</u>, Jesus tell-him, "Who finish see heaven? None—sh! Myself finish touch heaven. Long-ago desert, Moses snake lift-up (cl:s,s), same must myself lift-me-up, they look-at-me, believe, live forever. Yes, God love world so-much, his only Son he give, for-for? Any person believe~accept Son, that person die not; he live forever. Son God send for world punish? No. Son save world, God want."

Gospel his Lord.

All Saints

BOOK OF REVELATION (7:2–4, 9–14)

Myself, John, I see angel, east, come (cl:1), God his seal (fs and sign) hold. There angels four, they have power land, sea ruin can. Angel, he shout, "Destroy land, sea, trees, suspend; first servants his God seal (cl:f on forehead)." Seal++ altogether how many? 144,000 from every Israel group++. Finish, I see people hordes, count impossible, every country, color skin, language, hordes. They stand face-to-face throne, there Jesus (name Lamb). #ALL have clothes white, leaf palm they hold. They cry-out, "Save comes from God, himself sit there throne, and from Jesus." #ALL (1) angels, (2) leaders, (3) four living things, #ALL kneel++, worship God, say, "Amen (in palm)! Praise, glory, wise, thanks, honor, power, strong give-to our God forever and ever, Amen!" One leader question-me, "Those people white clothes—who? From where?" I answer, "You know. I don't-know." He tell-me, "Those people stubborn~continue, no-matter awful trouble, suffer. Their clothes they wash in blood from him lamb—now white, clean."

Word his Lord.

RESPONSORIAL PSALM (24:1–2, 3–4, 5–6)

Lord, we your people, your face wish see.

Lord control earth whole / #ALL people he control
Earth, he establish it / ocean, river, he make.

Lord his mountain, who climb, who? / his holy place stand, who?
That-one sin none, heart pure / worthless things, he hate.

That-one, Lord bless-him will / God save-him
Same #ALL people they obey God / his face they search-for.

FIRST LETTER OF JOHN (3:1–3)

Father love us, wow! He name-us his children. We his children true~work. But people here world understand not—why? Jesus they don't-know. Cherish friend, we true God his children now; but future, what? Know-nothing. We know-that happen Jesus come (cl:1) again, we become same-as-him. See himself (hon) will we. Every person, suppose future see Christ hope, keep themselves pure continue, same-as Christ, himself pure.

Word his Lord.

GOSPEL ACCLAMATION

Alleluia

Lord says, You work++, tired, come-here
Rest, I give-you.

HOLY GOSPEL ACCORDING TO MATTHEW (5:1–12)

Jesus see people hordes, mountain walk-up (cl:v-legs), sit, disciples sit-around-him (cl:crooked 4,4). Jesus teach, "You people depend-on God, bless you, why? Kingdom heaven he give-you will. You people sad, grief, bless you—God kind-to-you. You people humble, bless you—land take-up control will. You hunger, thirst for judge~fair, bless you—satisfy will. You mercy-out, bless you—God mercy-you. Your heart cherish God, bless you—see God will you. You bring peace, bless you—name-you children his God. You live right; wrong hit suffer, persecute-you, bless you, why? Future you, heaven, connect. Suppose you follow me, wrong happen people insult-you, hate-you lie~gossip about you, bless you. Celebrate happy! Why? There heaven have wonderful <u>reward</u> give-you."

Gospel his Lord.

Dedication of the Lateran Basilica

BOOK OF THE PROPHET EZEKIEL (47:1–2, 8–9, 12)

There temple, angel carry-me. Door, I see water flow-toward-me, east (toward me)—temple front, east (toward me). Water flow-to-left, south. Angel lead-me (r) north gate, out, come-around-to-front (cl:1,1). Water I see flow-to-left. Angel tell-me, quote, "That water flow where? Ocean, flow-into. Ocean, its water salt, water flow-into, become clean, <u>fresh</u>, salt dissolve. River flow, cause grow++ animal, plant, fish, various. Flow, ocean enter, become clean. Trees, fruit, grow plenty. Leaves green, fruit delicious, sour never. Every-month, new fruit, why? Temple water flow. Fruit eat, delicious; leaves, make medicine."

Word his Lord.

RESPONSORIAL PSALM (46:2–3, 5–6, 8–9)

God his city have water~river, happy; God himself live there.

God himself give-me protect, mighty / time-period trouble, he help-me
Earth messed-up, no matter, we afraid not / mountain break-down, no-matter.

Have river, itself cause God city happy / God himself live there
City, God there middle / time sunrise, God help-it.

Lord himself here with us / God himself defend us
Come-here! God his actions see / wonderful things he action here earth.

SECOND LETTER OF PAUL TO THE CORINTHIANS (3:9c–11, 16–17)

Brother~sister, you-all compare house. God teach-me, help-me build wise. First, support-support I establish, flat (cl:b,b). Other people build there. Understand, build careful must, why? Have support-support only-one, that-one Jesus Christ. Other place build, worthless.

?? Know-that yourself God his temple? His Holy Spirit live in you. Suppose temple, person destroy, God see, destroy-him. Why? Temple holy, means yourself holy.

Word his Lord.

GOSPEL ACCLAMATION

Alleluia

This house I choose, bless.
Live there forever, will I.

HOLY GOSPEL ACCORDING TO JOHN (2:13–22)

Jew <u>Passover</u> near-future, near, Jerusalem Jesus go-to. Temple arrive, people see—they #do-do? Cow, sheep, bird sell; other people sit, money budget share. Jesus make same <u>whip</u>, string, crack-whip, tables overturn, money coins roll-away. Jesus bawl-out, "Away! My Father house, you change sell place. Finish!" Apostles remember Bible predict, quote, "Your house I enthusiastic cherish"—oh-I-see. Jew people question, "Your authority action all-this, where? Proof where?" Jesus answer, "This (hon) temple destroy, 3-days later I set-up again." (Jews) "This temple build require 46 years, but you 3-days set up? Sick you!" True, Jesus mean what temple? His body. Later, Jesus die, resurrect finish, apostles remember, look-back Jesus story, oh-I-see, believe.

Gospel his Lord.

IMMACULATE CONCEPTION

BOOK OF GENESIS (3:9–15, 20)

Tree, fruit, <u>Adam</u> eat; finish, Lord God call-out, "Where you?" (Adam) "You here <u>garden</u>, I hear, but afraid—why? I naked, hide." (God) "Oh-I-see. Who inform-you naked you? Maybe fruit you eat from tree that-one I prohibit?" (Adam) "Woman you put-here, fruit she give-me, so I eat." Lord God question-to woman, "Fruit you eat—why?" (Woman) "Snake, he butter-up-hit. I eat." Snake, Lord God tell-him, "You awful action—punish what? From-now-on, #ALL other animals reject-you; you must crawl-like-snake (cl:1), soil eat. Self, woman, enemy. Your children, her children, enemy. Her son <u>foot</u> you bite (left bite right); he (right stomp on left)." <u>Adam</u> name wife <u>Eve</u>—why? She mother for every person from-now-on.

Word his Lord.

RESPONSORIAL PSALM (98:1, 2–3, 3–4)

New song sign-ASL-to Lord; he finish wonderful action.

New song sign-ASL-to Lord / he finish wonderful action
His right hand win succeed / himself mighty.

#ALL people Lord himself save / #ALL countries his judge~fair
he show-around
He up-to-now kind, faithful / people Israel he cherish.

People all-over earth / finish see God save us
#ALL country sing happy for Lord / sign-ASL, praise.

LETTER OF PAUL TO THE EPHESIANS (1:3–6, 11–12)

Praise God, himself father <u>of</u> our Lord Jesus Christ. God give-us every spirit blessing from heaven—how? Give-us Christ. Before God make world, before, he choose us become holy, sin none. Past, he plan adopt us become his children—he think-self—for-for? Want #ALL people praise him because he love us, give us Christ. So, God choose us with Christ, connect; God cause everything happen++ follow his plan, his want; his glory he want us praise—how? Believe, trust Christ.

Word his Lord.

GOSPEL ACCLAMATION

Alleluia

Hello, Mary, yourself inspire grace, Lord touch-you
Bless you than other women.

HOLY GOSPEL ACCORDING TO LUKE (1:26–38)

Angel name <u>Gabriel</u>, God send touch town name <u>Nazareth</u>, visit virgin, herself near-future marry man name <u>Joseph</u>, himself family <u>David</u> descend. Virgin, her name <u>Mary</u>. Angel come-down (cl:1), said, "Celebrate! God with you, bless you special want!" She confused, not understand. (Angel) "Fear, wave-no. God satisfy you. You will pregnant, born son, name-him Jesus. People honor-him, name-him Son <u>of</u> God Most High. Lord God give-him authority same David, his ancestor. He control people Israel forever; his control completed never."

Mary question, "How possible? I marry not-yet, me." (Angel) "Holy Spirit touch you will, power his God Most High inspire you. Your holy baby true~work son his God. Know-that <u>Elizabeth</u>, your cousin, herself old, now pregnant. People think she pregnant can't (^), but now sixth month pregnant. God expert action anything!" (Mary) "Serve Lord I willing. Go-ahead, happen same you recent story." Finish, angel leave~dissolve.

Gospel his Lord.

GLOSSARY OF SIGNS

Almost-nothing	F-handshape, index and thumb touch tip of nose, then wrist turns inward sharply, ending palm-forward
Appropriate	Right-right
Away-they-go	Natural "shooing" motion, one or both hands, bent B handshape, palms down, sweep to palm-forward in the direction of the shooing
Beginning-to-end	Left hand open 5, palm in, right hand B handshape, palm left, starts at left thumb and sweeps down to baby finger, ending palm-up
Big-brains	cup handshape on both hands, placed at forehead one in front of the other
Can't (^)	As the index finger crooks into an X, it turns sharply inward
Cl	Classifier; use hands to show shape and usage of named item
Cover-up	Left 5 hand palm up, right 5 hand palm down; right moves backward over left, as if smoothing something over
Dash	Left hand flat, palm down, right hand flat, palm up; right pal brushes against left palm as right moves up and outward toward right
Exchange-words	Open hands, palms up, move alternately back and forth between the two people who are exchanging words
Fine-wiggle	Fine, thumb against chest, fingers wiggle
Frequented	Left hand 1 handshape; right hand B handshape; palm in, fingers pointing to left hand 1; fingertips of B repeatedly move toward left 1 in circular motion; may actually touch
Fuss-back-and-forth	Thumbs and fingertips of both flat-O hands wiggle against each other while both hands move back and forth between the two people who are fussing
Get-by	Both hands open 8, palm in, close to face; hands circle alternately toward face, middle fingers touching lower lip
Good-riddance	Both hands palm out directionally, quickly close to flat-Os
Gotcha	U handshape moves in quick movement toward person who is being "got"
Grief	Heart-wring
Gulp	Throat-clutch—oops!
Halt	Open hand, palm out; natural gesture
Hands-off	Middle finger of open 8 hands brush something off both shoulders
Heart-express	Like "sign-ASL," but start close to the heart
Hey!	Wave hand up and down, as if getting someone's attention
Hm	Thoughtful gesture, rubbing chin
Holier-than-thou	Both hands at shoulders, palms out, fingers pointing up, ring fingers bent down at knuckle
Hosanna	Many variations. Try "alleluia" with H handshapes

Immerse	The "dunking" sign for baptism
Isaiah	Sign "prophet" using I handshape
Jump-at-chance	Right hand from C to S, snatches something off left palm
Kick-back	Crooked index fingers on both hands fall apart, representing legs hanging over the arms of an easy chair
Knock	Left hand 1 handshape, right hand knocks sharply on side of index finger
Know-nothing	O or F handshape bounces gently in front of forehead
Know-that	B hand at forehead, index touching forehead, bends sharply forward at wrist
Laid-back	"Casual"; both 5 hands, palms down, move together from left to right to left in relaxed manner
Learn-lesson	Fingertips of flat-O touch forehead, then hand opens and fingers slap forehead
Let's see	See-see
Little-story	"Story" signed with small double movement, "narrate"
Look-like	Face-same
Lose-temper	Blow-up; left hand S (see "put-him-there"); right hand 5 rises slowly
Make-me-sick	Right hand only signs "sick" but twists as it touches forehead
Mill-around	5-handshapes, one with fingers pointing up, the other pointing down, fingers wiggling, hand circle each other horizontally
Miss-the-point	Left hand 1, pointing up; right index snaps out toward left index as if to hit it, but instead misses and veers off to the left
Mooch	Both hands in "duck" handshape, right hand "bites" left, draws it toward self
More-than	The sign for "than"
Mull-over	Thumb and fingertips tap quickly and lightly together while whole hand moves in a very small circle in front of forehead
Next-to-her	Make "agent" sign (both flat hands, palms facing each other, move down slightly), then move both hands purposefully to the right and sign it again
#NG	N in the normal position; twist wrist inward so that the G is thumb up
No-wave	One or both 5-hands, palms forward, shake back and forth
(on fingers)	Left 5-hand, palm-in, fingers pointing right; right index points to fingertips one by one
Out-thumb	Natural gesture; looks like hitchhiking
Pah!	Succeed, signed once strongly
Phooey	Right hand palm forward swishes to palm-down in a natural gesture of dismissal
Priest~most	"Priest" with "est" ending

Promiscuity	Left hand 5, palm in; right hand bent-V sweeps across ends of left fingers from thumb to baby finger
Pull-in-head	Left hand C like cup; right hand S like a head; left C encircles right forearm, right arm moves down quickly, like a turtle pulling in its head
Put-him-there	S handshape, like grabbing a staff, movement directional
Recruit	Left hand 1 handshape; right hand bent-V hooks left 1 and draws it toward self
Ritzy	3 handshape, finger pointing up, thumb bumps up against chin
Same-around	Both hands Y handshape, palms down, thumbs almost touching; circle hands in wide horizontal arc
Same-as	Y handshape, palms forward, moves back and forth from left to right or between the things that are the same
Same-same	1 handshape on both hands, palms down; sides of index fingers touch, separate, move slightly to the right, and touch again
See-if	See-see
Set-up	Opposite of "collapse"; fingers lift to a tent shape
Shot-h	S handshape moves forward directionally and ends with sudden change to H handshape
Slick-talk	Both hands near mouth in flat-O handshape, one slightly in front of the other, palms up; thumbs slide across fingers (like "smooth") several times
So-what	Right hand, bent-B, palm in, backs of fingers under chin; hand flips forward and opens to palm in, fingers pointing straight up
Stand-strong	Looks like "tree" except right hand is a fist
Synagogue	S-y on wrist, like "church"
That's-all	Finish! Ending with hands at shoulders, palms forward
Tool-around	Open-8 hands, one pointing up, the other pointing down, circle in a series of horizontal loops
Trivial	"Nothing-to-it"; two F hands, palms out, shake horizontally
United-to	"Connect" and then shake it a little
Un-popular	Left hand 1; right hand 5 moves backward, away from the 1
Up-to-now	Same as "since," but bigger and slower
Well . . .	Natural gesture, both hands open in front of body, palms up
Whoa!	Claw handshape, palm in, moves back and forth in front of face
Whole-thing	The sign for "all"

INDEX OF SCRIPTURES

This comprehensive index covers all three volumes of Signing the Scriptures: years A, B, and C

Genesis
1:1—2:2 *61 A, 66 B, 66 C*
2:7–9, 3:1–7 *29 A*
2:18–24 *151 B*
3:9–15 *116 B*
3:9–15, 20 *3 A, 183 B, 190 C*
9:8–15 *30 B*
12:1–4a *32 A*
14:18–20 *100 C*
15:1–6, 21:1–3 *17 B*
15:5–12, 17–18 *31 C*
18:1–10 *136 C*
18:20–32 *138 C*
22:1–18 *62 A, 67 B, 67 C*
22:1–2, 9, 10–13, 15–18 *32 B*

Exodus
3:1–8, 13–15 *33 C*
12:1–8, 11–14 *51 A, 56 B, 55 C*
14:15—15:1 *63 A, 68 B, 68 C*
15:1–2, 3–4, 5–6, 17–18 *64 A, 69 B, 69 C*
16:2–4, 12–15 *133 B*
17:3–7 *34 A, 35 C, 36 B*
17:8–13 *165 C*
19:2–6a *114 A*
20:1–17 *34 B*
22:20–26 *153 A*
24:3–8 *98 B*
32:7–11, 13–14 *154 C*
34:4–6, 8–9 *91 A*

Leviticus
13:1–2, 44–46 *108 B*
19:1–2, 17–18 *106 A*

Numbers
6:22–27 *21 A, 21 B, 19 C*
11:25–29 *149 B*
21:4–9 *174 A, 177 B*

Deuteronomy
4:1–2, 6–8 *141 B*
4:32–34, 39–40 *96 B*
5:12–15 *114 B*
6:2–6 *159 B*
8:2–3, 14–16 *93 A*
11:18, 26–28, 32 *110 A*
18:15–20 *104 B*
26:4–10 *28 C*
30:10–14 *134 C*

Joshua
5:9a, 10–12 *38 C*
24:1–2, 15–17, 18 *139 B*

1 Samuel
1: 20–22, 24–28 *16 C*
3:3–10, 19 *100 B*
16:1, 6–7, 10–13 *37 A, 40 C*
16:6–7, 10–13 *41 B*
26:2, 7–9, 12–13, 22–23 *115 C*

2 Samuel
5:1–3 *175 C*
7:1–5, 8–12, 14, 16 *7 B*
12:7–10, 13 *124 C*

1 Kings
3:5, 7–12 *127 A*
8:41–43 *120 C*
17:10–16 *163 B*
17:17–24 *122 C*
19:4–8 *135 B*
19:9, 11–13 *131 A*
19:16, 19–21 *129 C*

2 Kings
4:8–11, 14–16 *118 A*
4:42–44 *131 B*
5:14–17 *163 C*

2 Chronicles
36:14–16, 19–23 *39 B*

Nehemiah
8:2–6, 8–10 *104 C*

2 Maccabees
7:1–2, 9–14 *171 C*

Job
7:1–4, 6–7 *106 B*
38:1, 8–11 *121 B*

Psalms
1 *113 C*
4 *80 B*
8 *98 C*
15 *141 B, 136 C*
16 *63 A, 75 A, 68 B, 163 B, 68 C, 129 C*
17 *171 C*
18 *153 A, 159 B*
19 *67 A, 34 B, 72 B, 149 B, 72 C, 104 C*
22 *43 A, 50 B, 84 B, 48 C*
23 *37 A, 78 A, 149 A, 161 A, 41 B, 129 B, 40 C*
24 *10 A, 164 A, 176 A, 167 B, 179 B, 177 C, 186 C*
25 *145 A, 30 B, 102 B, 1 C*
27 *87 A, 97 A, 31 C*
29 *25 A*
30 *65 A, 70 B, 123 B, 70 C, 81 C, 122 C*
31 *54 A, 110 A, 59 B, 59 C*
32 *108 B, 124 C*
33 *32 A, 62 A, 80 A, 67 B, 96 B, 155 B, 67 C, 143 C*
34 *168 A, 135 B, 137 B, 139 B, 171 B, 38 C, 167 C, 182 C*
40 *95 A, 100 B, 146 C*
41 *110 B*
42 *68 A, 73 B, 73 C*
45 *172 A, 174 B, 184 C*
46 *178 A, 181 B, 188 C*
47 *85 A, 88 B, 90 C*

50 *112 A*	118 *70 A, 71 A, 73 A, 75 B,*	**Isaiah**
51 *27 A, 29 A, 69 A, 27 B,*	*76 B, 78 B, 82 B, 75 C,*	2:1–5 *1 A*
44 B, 74 B, 27 C, 74 C	*76 C, 78 C*	5:1–7 *147 A*
154 C	119 *103 A, 127 A*	6:1–8 *110 C*
54 *108 A, 147 B*	121 *165 C*	7:10–14 *10 A*
63 *137 A, 157 A, 127 C*	122 *1 A, 175 C*	8:23—9:3 *97 A*
65 *122 A*	123 *125 B*	9:1–3, 5–6 *15 A, 13 B, 12 C*
66 *83 A, 131 C*	126 *157 B, 3 C, 43 C*	11:1–10 *5 A*
67 *21 A, 133 A, 21 B, 19 C,*	128 *19 A, 159 A, 151 B*	12:2–3, 4, 5–6 *66 A, 26 B,*
88 C	130 *40 A, 46 B, 116 B, 45 C*	*71 B, 5 C, 71 C*
68 *150 C*	131 *155 A, 39 B*	22:19–23 *135 A*
69 *116 A, 134 C*	138 *135 A, 110 C, 138 C*	25:6–10 *149 A*
71 *107 C*	139 *166 A, 169 B, 180 C*	35:1–6, 10 *8 A*
72 *5 A, 23 A, 23 B, 21 C*	145 *120 A, 129 A, 143 A,*	35:4–7 *143 B*
78 *174 A, 133 B, 177 B*	*131 B, 86 C, 169 C*	40:1–5, 9–11 *3 B, 23 C*
80 *147 A, 1 B, 7 C*	146 *8 A, 99 A, 143 B, 161 B,*	42:1–4, 6–7 *25 A, 25 B, 23 C*
81 *114 B*	*159 C*	43:16–21 *43 C*
84 *17 C*	147 *93 A, 106 B*	43:18–19, 21–22, 24b–25
85 *131 A, 3 B, 127 B*	**Proverbs**	*110 B*
86 *124 A*	8:22–31 *98 C*	45:1, 4–6 *151 A*
89 *12 A, 118 A, 7 B,*	9:1–6 *137 B*	49:1–6 *166 A, 169 B, 180 C*
10 B, 9 C	31:10–13, 19–20, 30–31	49:14–15 *108 A*
90 *153 B, 141 C, 152 C*	*159 A*	49:3, 5–6 *95 A*
91 *28 C*	**Ecclesiastes**	50:4–7 *43 A, 49 B, 48 C*
92 *119 B, 118 C*	1:2, 2:21–23 *141 C*	50:5–9a *145 B*
93 *165 B*	**Wisdom**	52:13—53:12 *53 A, 58 B,*
95 *34 A, 139 A, 36 B, 104 B,*	1:13–15, 2:23–24 *123 B*	*58 C*
35 C, 161 C	2:12, 17–20 *147 B*	52:7–10 *17 A, 15 B, 14 C*
96 *15 A, 151 A, 13 B, 12 C,*	6:12–16 *157 A*	53:10–11 *155 B*
102 C	7:7–11 *153 B*	54:5–14 *65 A, 70 B, 70 C*
97 *170 A, 173 B, 93 C*	9:13–18 *152 C*	55:1–11 *65 A, 25 B, 70 B,*
98 *3 A, 17 A, 15 B, 86 B,*	11:22–12:2 *169 C*	*70 C*
183 B, 14 C, 163 C, 173 C	12:13, 16–19 *124 A*	55:1–3 *129 A*
100 *114 A, 84 C*	18:6–9 *143 C*	55:10–11 *122 A*
103 *106 A, 141 A, 91 B, 33 C,*	**Sirach**	55:6–9 *143 A*
115 C	3:2–6, 12–14 *19 A, 17 B,*	56:1, 6–7 *133 A*
104 *61 A, 89 A, 66 B, 93 B,*	*16 C*	58:7–10 *101 A*
24 C, 66 C, 95 C	3:17–18, 20, 28–29 *150 C*	60:1–6 *23 A, 23 B, 21 C*
105 *18 B*	15:15–20 *103 A*	61:1–2, 10–11 *5 B*
107 *121 B*	27:4–7 *118 C*	62:1–5 *12 A, 10 B, 9 C,*
110 *100 C*	27:30—28:7 *141 A*	*102 C*
112 *101 A*	35:12–14, 16–18 *167 C*	63:16–17, 19; 64:2–7 *1 B*
113 *157 C*		66:10–14 *131 C*
116 *51 A, 32 B, 34 B, 56 B,*		66:18–21 *148 C*
98 B, 145 B, 55 C		
117 *120 C, 148 C*		

Jeremiah
1:4–5, 17–19 *107 C*
17:5–8 *113 C*
20:10–13 *116 A*
20:7–9 *137 A*
23:1–6 *129 B*
31:7–9 *157 B*
31:31–34 *44 B*
33:14–16 *1 C*
38:4–6, 8–10 *146 C*

Baruch
3:9–15, 32—4:4 *67 A, 72 B, 72 C*
5:1–9 *3 C*

Ezekiel
2:2–5 *125 B*
17:22–24 *119 B*
18:25–28 *145 A*
33:7–9 *139 A*
34:11–12, 15–17 *161 A*
36:16–17, 18–28 *68 A, 73 C*
36:16–28 *73 B*
37:12–14 *40 A, 45 C, 46 B*
47:1–2, 8–9, 12 *178 A, 181 B, 188 C*

Daniel
3:52, 53, 54, 55, 56 *91 A*
7:9–10, 13–14 *170 A, 173 B*
7:13–14 *165 B*
12:1–3 *163 B*

Hosea
2:16b, 17b, 21–22 *112 B*
6:3–6 *112 A*

Joel
2:12–18 *27 A, 28 B, 26 C*

Amos
6:1, 4–7 *159 C*
7:12–15 *127 B*
8:4–7 *157 C*

Jonah
3:1–5, 10 *102 B*

Micah
5:1–4 *7 C*

Habakkuk
1:2–3, 2:2–4 *161 C*

Zephaniah
2:3, 3:12–13 *99 A*
3:14–18 *5 C*

Zechariah
9:9–10 *120 A*
12:10–11 *127 C*

Malachi
1:14—2:2, 8–10 *155 A*
3:1–4 *164 A, 167 B, 177 C*
3:19–20 *173 C*

Matthew
1:1–25 *13 A, 11 B, 10 C*
1:18–24 *11 A*
2:1–12 *24 A, 24 B, 22 C*
2:13–15, 19–23 *20 A*
3:1–12 *6 A*
3:13–17 *26 A*
4:1–11 *30 A*
4:12–23 *98 A*
5:1–12 *100 A, 177 A, 180 B, 187 C*
5:13–16 *102 A*
5:17–37 *104 A*
5:38–48 *107 A*
6:1–6, 16–18 *28 A, 29 B, 27 C*
6:24–34 *109 A*
7:21–27 *111 A*
9:9–13 *113 A*
10:26–33 *117 A*
10:37–42 *119 A*
11:2–11 *9 A*
11:25–30 *121 A*
13:1–23 *123 A*
13:24–43 *125 A*
13:44–52 *128 A*
14:13–21 *130 A*
14:22–23 *132 A*
15:21–28 *134 A*
16:13–19 *169 A, 172 B, 183 C*
16:13–20 *136 A*
16:21–27 *138 A*
17:1–9 *33 A*
18:15–20 *140 A*
18:21–35 *142 A*
20:1–16 *144 A*
21:1–11 *43 A*
21:28–32 *146 A*
21:33–43 *148 A*
22:1–14 *150 A*
22:15–21 *152 A*
22:34–40 *154 A*
23:1–12 *156 A*
24:37–44 *2 A*
25:1–13 *158 A*
25:14–30 *160 A*
25:31–46 *162 A*
26:14—27:66 *44 A*
28:1–10 *70 A, 75 C*
28:16–20 *86 A, 97 B*

Mark
1:1–8 *4 B*
1:7–11 *27 B*
1:12–15 *31 B*
1:14–20 *103 B*
1:21–28 *105 B*
1:29–39 *107 B*
1:40–45 *109 B*
2:1–12 *111 B*
2:18–22 *113 B*
2:23–3:6 *115 B*
3:20–35 *117 B*
4:26–34 *120 B*
4:35–41 *122 B*
5:21–43 *124 B*
6:1–6 *126 B*
6:30–34 *130 B*
6:7–13 *128 B*
7:1–8, 14–15, 21–23 *142 B*
7:31–37 *144 B*
8:27–35 *146 B*
9:2–10 *171 A, 33 B, 174 B*
9:30–37 *148 B*
9:38–43, 45, 47–48 *150 B*

10:17–30 *154 B*
10:2–16 *152 B*
10:35–45 *156 B*
10:46–52 *158 B*
11:1–10 *49 B*
12:28–34 *160 B*
12:38–44 *162 B*
13:24–32 *164 B*
13:33–37 *2 B*
14:1—15:47 *51 B*
14:12–16, 22–26 *99 B*
16:1–7 *75 B*
16:15–20 *90 B*

Luke

1:1–4; 4:14–21 *106 C*
1:26–38 *4 A, 8 B, 184 B, 191 C*
1:39–45 *8 C*
1:39–56 *173 A, 176 B, 185 C*
1:46–48, 49–50, 53–54 *5 B*
1:57–66, 80 *167 A, 170 B, 181 C*
2:1–14 *16 A, 14 B, 13 C*
2:16–21 *22 A, 22 B, 20 C*
2:22–40 *165 A, 19 B, 168 B, 178 C*
2:41–52 *18 C*
3:1–6 *4 C*
3:10–18 *6 C*
3:15–16, 21–22 *25 C*
4:1–13 *29 C*
4:21–30 *108 C*
5:1–11 *111 C*
6:17, 20–26 *114 C*
6:27–38 *116 C*
6:39–45 *119 C*
7:1–10 *121 C*
7:11–17 *123 C*
7:36—8:3 *125 C*
9:11–17 *101 C*
9:18–24 *128 C*
9:28–36 *32 C*
9:51–62 *130 C*
10:1–12, 17–20 *132 C*
10:25–37 *135 C*
10:38–42 *137 C*

11:1–13 *139 C*
12:13–21 *142 C*
12:32–48 *144 C*
12:49–53 *147 C*
13:1–9 *34 C*
13:22–30 *149 C*
14:1, 7–14 *151 C*
14:25–33 *153 C*
15:1–3, 11–32 *39 C*
15:1–32 *155 C*
16:1–13 *158 C*
16:19–31 *160 C*
17:11–19 *164 C*
17:5–10 *162 C*
18:1–8 *166 C*
18:9–14 *168 C*
19:1–10 *170 C*
19:28–40 *48 C*
20:27–38 *172 C*
21:25–28, 34–36 *2 C*
21:5–19 *174 C*
22:14–23:56 *49 C*
23:35–43 *176 C*
24:13–35 *76 A*
24:35–48 *81 B*
24:46–53 *92 C*

John

1:1–18 *18 A, 16 B, 15 C*
1:29–34 *96 A*
1:35–42 *101 B*
1:6–8, 19–28 *6 B*
2:1–12 *103 C*
2:13–22 *179 A, 182 B, 189 C*
2:13–25 *35 B*
3:13–17 *175 A, 178 B*
3:14–21 *40 B*
3:16–18 *92 A*
4:5–42 *35 A, 37 B, 36 C*
6:1–15 *132 B*
6:24–35 *134 B*
6:41–51 *136 B*
6:51–58 *94 A, 138 B*
6:60–69 *140 B*
8:1–11 *44 C*
9:1–41 *38 A, 42 B, 41 C*
10:1–10 *79 A*

10:11–18 *83 B*
10:27–30 *85 C*
11:1–45 *41 A, 47 B, 46 C*
12:12–16 *49 B*
12:20–33 *45 B*
13:1–15 *52 A, 57 B, 56 C*
13:31–35 *87 C*
14:1–12 *81 A*
14:15–16, 23–26 *97 C*
14:15–21 *84 A*
14:23–29 *89 C*
15:1–8 *85 B*
15:26–27, 16:12–15 *95 B*
15:9–17 *87 B*
16:12–15 *99 C*
17:1–11 *88 A*
17:11b–19 *92 B*
17:20–26 *94 C*
18:1–19:42 *55 A, 60 B, 60 C*
18:33–37 *166 B*
20:1–9 *72 A, 77 B, 77 C*
20:19–23 *90 A, 95 B, 97 C*
20:19–31 *74 A, 79 B, 79 C*
21:1–19 *82 C*

Acts

1:1–11 *85 A, 88 B, 90 C*
1:12–14 *87 A*
1:15–17, 20a, 20c–26 *91 B*
2:1–11 *89 A, 93 B, 95 C*
2:14, 22–33 *75 A*
2:14, 36–41 *78 A*
2:42–47 *73 A*
3:13–15, 17–19 *80 B*
4:32–35 *78 B*
4:8–12 *82 B*
5:12–16 *78 C*
5:27–32, 40–41 *81 C*
6:1–7 *80 A*
7:55–60 *93 C*
8:5–8, 14–17 *83 A*
9:26–31 *84 B*
10:25–26, 34–35, 44–48 *86 B*
10:34–38 *25 A, 27 B, 25 C*
10:34, 37–43 *71 A, 76 B, 76 C*

191

12:1–11 *168 A, 171 B, 182 C*
13:14, 43–52 *84 C*
13:16–17, 22–25 *12 A, 10 B, 10 C*
13:22–26 *167 A, 170 B, 181 C*
14:21–27 *86 C*
15:1–2, 22–29 *88 C*

Romans

1:1–7 *10 A*
3:21–25, 28 *110 A*
4:18–25 *113 A*
5:1–2, 5–8 *34 A, 36 B, 35 C*
5:1–5 *98 C*
5:12–15 *117 A*
5:12–19 *30 A*
5:6–11 *114 A*
6:3–11 *69 A, 74 B, 74 C*
6:3–4, 8–11 *118 A*
8:14–17 *97 B*
8:18–23 *122 A*
8:26–27 *125 A*
8:28–30 *128 A*
8:31–34 *33 B*
8:35, 37–39 *129 A*
8:8–11 *40 A, 46 B, 45 C*
8:8–17 *96 C*
8:9, 11–13 *120 A*
9:1–5 *131 A*
10:8–13 *29 C*
11:13–15, 29–32 *133 A*
11:33–36 *136 A*
12:1–2 *137 A*
13:11–14 *2 A*
13:8–10 *139 A*
14:7–9 *142 A*
15:4–9 *6 A*
16:25–27 *8 B*

1 Corinthians

1:1–3 *95 A*
1:10–13, 17 *97 A*
1:22–25 *35 B*
1:26–31 *99 A*
1:3–9 *1 B*
2:1–5 *101 A*
2:6–10 *103 A*
3:16–23 *106 A*
4:1–5 *108 A*
5:6b–8 *72 A, 77 B, 77 C*
6:13–15, 17–20 *101 B*
7:29–31 *102 B*
7:32–35 *104 B*
9:16–19, 22–23 *106 B*
10:1–6, 10–12 *34 C*
10:16–17 *93 A*
10:31—11:1 *108 B*
11:23–26 *52 A, 57 B, 56 C, 100 C*
12:12–30 *105 C*
12:3–7, 12–13 *90 A, 94 B, 96 C*
12:31—13:13 *107 C*
12:4–11 *102 C*
15:1–11 *111 C*
15:12, 16–20 *113 C*
15:20–26 *172 A*
15:20–26, 28 *162 A*
15:20–27 *175 B, 183 C*
15:45–49 *116 C*
15:54–58 *118 C*

2 Corinthians

1:18–22 *110 B*
3:1b–6 *112 B*
3:9c–11, 16–17 *179 A, 182 B, 189 C*
4:13—5:1 *116 B*
4:6–11 *114 B*
5:14–17 *121 B*
5:17–21 *38 C*
5:20—6:2 *28 A, 29 B, 27 C*
5:6–10 *119 B*
8:7, 9, 13–15 *123 B*
12:7–10 *125 B*
13:11–13 *91 A*

Galatians

1:1–2, 6–10 *120 C*
1:11–19 *123 C*
2:16, 19–21 *124 C*
3:26–29 *127 C*
4:4–7 *21 A, 21 B, 19 C*
5:1, 13–18 *129 C*
5:16–25 *93 B*
6:14–18 *131 C*

Ephesians

1:17–23 *86 A, 89 B, 91 C*
1:3–14 *127 B*
1:3–6, 11–12 *3 A, 183 B, 191 C*
2:13–18 *129 B*
2:4–10 *40 B*
3:2–3, 5–6 *23 A, 23 B, 21 C*
4:1–13 *89 B*
4:1–6 *131 B*
4:17, 20–24 *133 B*
4:30—5:2 *135 B*
5:15–20 *137 B*
5:21–32 *139 B*
5:8–14 *38 A, 41 C, 42 B*

Philippians

1:20–24 *143 A*
1:4–6, 8–11 *4 C*
2:1–11 *145 A*
2:6–11 *44 A, 175 A, 50 B, 178 B, 49 C*
3:17—4:1 *32 C*
3:8–14 *43 C*
4:12–14, 19–20 *149 A*
4:4–7 *5 C*
4:6–9 *148 A*

Colossians

1:12–20 *175 C*
1:15–20 *134 C*
1:24–28 *136 C*
2:12–14 *139 C*
3:1–4 *71 A, 76 B, 76 C*
3:1–5, 9–11 *141 C*
3:12–21 *19 A, 18 B, 17 C*

1 Thessalonians

1:1–5 *152 A*
1:5–10 *153 A*
2:7–9, 13 *155 A*

3:12—4:2 *1 C*
4:13–18 *157 A*
5:1–6 *159 A*
5:16–24 *5 B*

2 Thessalonians
1:11—2:2 *170 C*
2:16–35 *171 C*
3:7–12 *173 C*

1 Timothy
1:12–17 *154 C*
2:1–8 *157 C*
6:11–16 *159 C*

2 Timothy
1:6–8, 13–14 *161 C*
1:8b–10 *32 A*
2:8–13 *163 C*
3:14—4:2 *165 C*
4:6–8, 16–18 *179 A, 172 B, 167 C, 183 C*

Titus
2:11–14 *16 A, 14 B, 13 C*
2:11–14; 3:4–7 *24 C*

Philemon
9–10, 12–17 *152 C*

Hebrews
1:1–6 *17 A, 15 B, 14 C*
2:14–18 *164 A, 167 B, 177 C*
2:9–11 *152 B*
4:12–13 *153 B*
4:14–16 *155 B*
4:14–16, 5:7–9 *54 A, 59 B, 59 C*
5:1–6 *157 B*
5:7–9 *44 B*
7:23–28 *159 B*
9:11–15 *98 B*
9:24–28 *161 B*
9:24–28, 10:19–23 *91 C*
10:11–14, 18 *163 B*
10:5–10 *7 C*
11:1–2, 8–19 *143 C*
11:8, 11–12, 17–19 *18 B*
12:1–4 *146 C*
12:18–19, 22–24 *150 C*
12:5–7, 11–13 *148 C*

James
1:17–18, 21b–22, 27 *141 B*
2:1–5 *143 B*
2:14–18 *145 B*
3:16—4:3 *147 B*
5:1–6 *152 B*
5:7–10 *8 A*

1 Peter
1:17–21 *76 A*
1:3–9 *73 A*
2:20–25 *79 A*
2:4–9 *81 A*
3:15–18 *84 A*
3:18–22 *30 B*
4:13–16 *87 A*

2 Peter
1:16–19 *170 A*
1:16–19 *173 B*
3:8–14 *3 B*

1 John
2:1–5a *80 B*
3:1–2 *82 B*
3:1–2, 21–24 *17 C*
3:1–3 *177 A, 180 B, 187 C*
3:18–24 *85 B*
4:11–16 *92 B*
4:7–10 *87 B*
5:1–6 *78 B*
5:1–9 *26 B*

Revelation
1:5–8 *167 B*
1:9–13, 17–19 *78 C*
5:11–14 *81 C*
7:2–4, 9–14 *176 A, 179 B, 186 C*
7:9, 14–17 *85 C*
11:19a; 12:1–6, 10 *172 A, 175 B, 184 C*
21:1–5 *87 C*
21:10–14, 22–23 *89 C*
22:12–14, 15–17, 20 *93 C*

BX
2003
.A5
A44
2003
Year B